The New Era of the CCO

The New Era of the CCO

The Essential Role of Communication in a Volatile World

Edited by
Roger Bolton, Don W. Stacks, and Eliot Mizrachi

BEP BUSINESS EXPERT PRESS

The New Era of the CCO: *The Essential Role of Communication in a Volatile World*

First published in 2018 by
Business Expert Press, LLC
222 East 46th Street, New York, NY 10017
www.businessexpertpress.com

ISBN-13: 978-1-63157-535-8 (paperback)
ISBN-13: 978-1-63157-536-5 (e-book)

Business Expert Press Public Relations Collection

Collection ISSN: 2157-345X (print)
Collection ISSN: 2157-3476 (electronic)

Cover and interior design by Exeter Premedia Services Private Ltd., Chennai, India

First edition: 2018

10 9 8 7 6 5 4 3 2 1

Printed in the United States of America.

Abstract

The role of the Chief Communication Officer (CCO) in today's enterprise has dramatically changed over the past 30 years. Once focused on getting news out to media outlets, today's CCO has become an integral part of any enterprise—company, corporation, governmental, and nongovernmental entity. Today's CCO is responsible for internal and external communication, with creating and implementing communication strategies that help mold enterprise mission, vision, value, and character, and with building enterprise reputation through stakeholder engagement. As a part of the "C-Suite," the CCO must understand not only the psychology and sociology of the business, but also the role that she has in informing the C-Suite and the Chief Executive Officer what internal and external stakeholders are thinking and how this may affect corporate image in terms of credibility, confidence, trust, relationship, and reputation. In short, the new CCO must understand both the science and the art of communication and apply that knowledge to advancing her enterprise's goals and objectives through a faster and ever-larger-reaching set of media.

Keywords

Arthur W. Page Society, character, chief communication officer, mission, stakeholder, value, vision

Contents

Foreword

There is nothing permanent, except change.
—Heraclitus, Greek philosopher

If you are a professional engaged in the field of communication, or a business leader whose aim is to engender the public's trust and sustain your company's ability to operate in a world of evolving expectations, then *The New Era of the CCO: The Essential Role of Communication in a Volatile World* is a must read.

Let's be clear at the outset that "communication" does not mean "speaking at" various audiences, and "public relations" has nothing to do with spin. The chief communication officer (CCO) of today's top enterprises leads by establishing a corporate character, the unique and differentiating identity—mission, purpose, values, culture, business model, and strategy—that permeates the enterprise and informs everything it does and says. Around that character, enterprises are able to authentically engage stakeholders, earning their trust, support, and advocacy. To achieve this, the communication function undertakes analytical activities that guide the effective engagement of each stakeholder group—investors, customers, business partners, communities, employees, regulators, and so forth—all of whom influence the success or failure of the enterprise. Mere talk carries no weight today; heightened transparency dictates that actions do the speaking, and relationships, even partnerships of sorts, must be built around areas of mutual interest.

Nonetheless, great care must be given to what is said, how it is said, when it is said, and to whom it is said, especially in an era where near instantaneous reactions will manifest in the financial sector and on social media, as well as news outlets. Channels of communication must already be in place, not an afterthought, if a quick official response is to be credible.

In a real sense, *The New Era of the CCO* is a book about change and its increasingly rapid pace. It presents a convincing case about the central role that communication—and, more specifically, the CCO—plays in helping companies navigate a global business environment that is characterized by constantly evolving and disruptive technologies, shifting demographics and political trends, and emboldened and activist stakeholders.

As a result of these changes, the stakes for today's communicators, and the enterprises they represent, have never been higher. Foreshadowing these shifting expectations, the Arthur W. Page Society has produced a collection of reports and white papers over the past decade that explore a new model for enterprise communication. This model takes a closer look at the importance of culture and authenticity in conveying that enterprise's purpose and character, and examines how the technology and data revolution is transforming every aspect of communication and stakeholder engagement. Most recently, in 2016, the Page Society published a new report entitled *The New CCO*, which is its most detailed take to date on the role of the CCO and the corporate communication function.

The New Era of the CCO offers the Society's most comprehensive view of the forces that are transforming the field of communication. No other book offers more informed advice, from the world's leading enterprise and academic communicators, on the actions its readers can take to lead in this new reality.

Regardless of your role, you will learn from the insights, examples, case studies, and forward thinking advanced by this book's authors. Their writing will expand your view of the corporate communication function in an era of radical transparency and empowered stakeholders. They will also alter the way in which you approach your job—and the ways in which you apply the practice of enterprise communication—going forward.

The insights, case studies, and lessons offered here are not theoretical; they are real. Readers will come away understanding why it is essential that they gain a keener grasp of local norms and sensitivities, a greater sense of how to navigate varied political, regulatory, and socioeconomic challenges, and a greater ability to lead in a volatile world.

—David Samson
General Manager, Public Affairs, Chevron
Chairman, Arthur W. Page Society (2016 to 2018)

Introduction

Marcia DiStaso

The New Era of the CCO: The Essential Role of Communication in a Volatile World provides an overview of the increasingly critical contributions of corporate communication and the role of Chief Communication Officers (CCOs) in enterprise success. Through discussions supported by published research and professional experiences, the authors in this book build on previous Arthur W. Page Society thought leadership reports to bring readers a comprehensive look at the role of the CCO.

The 2016 Page Society report *The New CCO: Transforming Enterprises in a Changing World* begins with the statement "The CCO of today is at a critical inflection point." The current state of rapid change obfuscates the future plans of CCOs. The chapters in *The New Era of the CCO* take the reader on a journey in an effort to help navigate the current landscape while prompting thought about the future. To accomplish this, the book is divided into three main parts and 10 chapters.

Part I: New Realities of Enterprise Communications

The chapter "The Changing Business Landscape" written by Tina McCorkindale, Aedhmar Hynes, and Raymond Kotcher is an excellent start to the book with a comprehensive overview of the field. The authors describe the business landscape, the rise of technology, societal changes, health care, and the environment.

Chapter 2, "The Evolving Corporate Communication Function," by Paul Argenti, Maril MacDonald, and Sean O'Neill examines the changes in contemporary enterprise communication. The focus of this chapter provides a historical perspective of the CCO role. The authors explain how the role has evolved to include an increased focus on integration, collaboration, and globalization.

"The Trust Imperative" is the third chapter, written by Richard Edelman, Stephen A. Greyser, E. Bruce Harrison, and Tom Martin. They explain how the rapid pace of innovation, along with other factors, has led to amplified uncertainty and decreased trust. "Tell the truth" and "Prove it with action"—the first two Arthur W. Page Principles—are just as important and valued today as when they were first written years ago.

Part II: Building Belief

Chapter 4, "Managing the Corporate Character of the Enterprise: Identity, Purpose, Culture, and Values," by Shannon A. Bowen, Ginger Hardage, and Wendi Strong explains the importance of corporate character and how an enterprise's identity comes from its mission, vision, and purpose. They succinctly point out that successful CCOs serve as the corporate conscience, bring purpose to life, and institutionalize their values.

Chapter 5, "Stakeholder Engagement—Creating and Sustaining Advocacy," by Michael Fernandez, Matthew Gonring, and Sally Benjamin Young provides an in-depth look at stakeholders. The authors explain the historical approaches to stakeholders, along nine insights and six steps to establishing *authentic* stakeholder engagement. The main takeaway is that corporate character should be a driver, a guidepost, and a metric for building culture and effective relationships.

Part III: The New Role of Communications in the Enterprise

Charlotte R. Otto, Gary Sheffer, and Donald K. Wright wrote the sixth chapter titled "The Changing and Expanding Foundational Role of the CCO." They begin with a look at the foundational role of the CCO and then explain the increased scope, importance, and intensity of the CCO. This includes discussion about the key areas of being a strategic business leader and counselor, a steward of reputation, and an effective communicator.

Chapter 7, "Total Integration: Working Across the C-Suite," by James S. O'Rourke, IV, James Spangler, and Richard Woods answers the question, "Why integration is important." It is through integration that CCOs gain the understanding and ability necessary to activate and align corporate character and manage risk. Furthermore, becoming the valued and trusted enterprise officer enhances CCO influence within the C-Suite.

In Chapter 8, "Building an Enterprise Digital Engagement System," Terence (Terry) Flynn, Jon Iwata, and Alan Marks address the technological challenges impacting CCOs today. The intersection of data, technology, and people formed the basis for the three steps the authors identified for building a digital engagement system, which is destined to be the primary stakeholder engagement platform of the future.

Chapter 9, "Skills and Capabilities of the Modern CCO," by Mark Bain, W. Timothy Coombs, and Bob Feldman addresses the communication, interpersonal, and management/leadership skills critical for today's CCO. Ultimately, multidimensional skills are necessary for the CCOs of today.

Finally, Chapter 10, "The New Reality" by Roger Bolton, Jennifer Prosek, and Don W. Stacks, provides guidance for CCOs in our constantly evolving environment. The stakes have never been higher and this chapter concludes the book with a critical call to action for CCOs.

The book also includes an impressive list of case studies from the following companies:

HEINEKEN (Chapter 2)
General Motors (Chapter 3)
USAA (Chapter 4)
Southwest Airlines (Chapter 4)
Lundbeck (Chapter 5)
Ford Motor Company (Chapter 6)
AECOM (Chapter 6)
General Electric (Chapter 6)
Capital One (Chapter 7)
Navistar (Chapter 7)
Tesoro (Chapter 9)

In *The New Era of the CCO: The Essential Role of Communication in a Volatile World* we sought to provide a solid resource for both communication and general business leaders and everyone from students to professionals. This was not an easy task, so we began with a strong foundation of many years of Page Society thought leadership. Furthermore, we have an impressive collection of top academic and enterprise communicators who as chapter authors brought the topics to life and provided examples from their varied experiences. I agree with Dave Sampson, who said in his foreword, "No other book offers more informed advice."

CHAPTER 1

The Changing Business Landscape

Tina McCorkindale, Aedhmar Hynes, and Raymond Kotcher

We are undergoing a revolution in human communication.

In less time than it took read that sentence—a single second—people around the world sent 2.5 million e-mails and 193,000 text messages, added 219,000 posts to Facebook and 729 to Instagram, viewed 125,833 YouTube videos, and tweeted 7,259 messages (internetlivestats.com 2016; Coats 2016; webpagefx.com 2016).

Every day, 2.5 quintillion bytes of data are created—so much that 90 percent of the data in the world today has been created in the last two years alone, according to analysts' estimates (IBM 2016c). Much of this data is generated by individuals and captured by machines. The ability to access and understand this data from the "Internet of Things" is becoming a competitive differentiator for businesses. Think of all the data that enterprises[1] collect about their customers—the difference between those who make sense of these data through analytics to improve the customer experience and those who will not be a primary determinate of those who succeed in business and those who fail in the years to come.

---

[1] As noted earlier, we use the term "enterprise" to mean large businesses and/or corporations that have large local, regional, national, and global subsidiaries. This is not to demean smaller organizations, who often have the same communication concerns and problems, but not to the same scale.

However, this is about more than just data and how we communicate.[2] It is not just a revolution in human communication, but also one in the human experience.

The world's balance of power is being transformed. There is a shift in the structure of the world's demography. Millions are on the move from the Middle East to Europe, and across Eurasia and the African continent. Access to resources is becoming challenging, including fundamental human needs and rights, such as clean water, health care, nutrition, education, and equality. People are seeking and demanding transparency, integrity, and higher purpose from institutions everywhere.

Amidst this all-encompassing change, taking place at the speed of light, how does an enterprise succeed? For what changes in the business landscape do leaders need to be prepared?

In their *CEO Report*, Said Business School at Oxford University and Heidrick & Struggles (2015) reported chief executive officers (CEOs) are dealing with a business environment marked with uncertainty and change. CEOs said they value "ripple intelligence," early warning systems much like the ripples on a pond, which sharpen as they learn to embrace the power of doubt. CEOs reported believing in an authentic sense of purpose for their organizations, and alignment in order to achieve it. Given intense stakeholder[3] scrutiny, CEOs are looking for new ways to communicate effectively as old models become outdated; there are more audiences, languages, and communication channels than ever before.

In 2015, KPMG International published its *Global CEO Outlook* that surveyed more than 1,200 CEOs on the global economic challenges for the next three years, as well as their thinking on strategies for responding to those challenges. Growth is a top priority, even as CEOs navigate the vicissitudes of inconsistent regulations from country to country.

---

[2] Throughout this volume, the term "communication" is used when discussing the role of communication strategies and its function in the enterprise. Communications refer to the actual channels employed in executing those strategies (such as written, spoken, and broadcast).

[3] Stakeholders include anyone who has a stake in the activities of an enterprise (e.g., employees, customers, investors, communities, public interest groups, and regulators).

Competitive threats not only from traditional incumbents, but also from new entrants, business models, and disruptive technologies represent increasingly challenging threats. Being relevant to customers, and maintaining both employee and customer loyalty, is critically important. In this digital age, cybersecurity and protecting private information are critical.

Similarly, PwC's *19th Global CEO Survey* (2016) of 1,400 CEOs reports that stakeholders have greater expectations operating in society with transparency and trust at the core. The CEOs reported a need for consistent and dependable communication, as well as the need to apply data and analytics to more effectively measure and express performance around business and strategy, purpose, and values. Nearly half said they are rethinking how they communicate "brand."

Today's business environment is going through changes on a level not seen since the Industrial Revolution. From technological to societal change, this upheaval presents CEOs and their Chief Communication Officers (CCOs) with numerous challenges: start-ups reinventing traditional business models, new ways of working, changing ways people interact with enterprises, and an increasingly diverse workforce. But where there are challenges, there are always opportunities. The question leaders need to ask themselves is, "Do I want my business to be a disruptor or disrupted?" Organizations that succeed will be those that thrive and adapt to this new environment, and CEOs need to be aware of multiple factors that will transform the landscape.

Business Landscape

Transparency, the primacy of the stakeholder, and engagement with purpose are all critical forces driving business and communication in this day of unremitting change.

Transparency

This is the age of transparency, or what *The Economist* (2014) calls the "openness revolution." Stakeholders are demanding greater accountability and an end to "corporate secrecy" (p. 2) multinationals are being "forced" to reveal more information about themselves. According to *The Economist*, three forces are driving this: (1) governments demanding greater accountability; (2) the power of investigative journalism; and (3) the sophistication of nongovernmental organizations (NGOs).

In the Starbucks shareholder meeting in 2014, then CEO Howard Schultz emphasized how the world needs leadership more than ever, and companies have a responsibility to use the power of their businesses to do good in the world. He said, "The currency of leadership is trust and transparency" (p. 8). With such exogenous forces impacting the enterprise, transparency can no longer be borne out of practical necessity. It must be a deeply held value. *Opacity comes with costs.*

A survey by EY and the Boston College Center for Corporate Citizenship (2013) of senior corporate professionals who were familiar with their organization's sustainability efforts found that transparency with stakeholders was a key motivation for enterprises to disclose information, and most respondents reported business benefits as a result of their company reporting efforts. According to Iwata and O'Neill (2016, p. 4), "highly engaged stakeholders, empowered by social media and demanding of greater transparency, pose new challenges for protecting brand and reputation." As reported in the Arthur W. Page monograph, *The Authentic Enterprise* (2007), power continues to shift to the stakeholder, and the demand for transparency will continue to grow.

The Primacy of Stakeholders

In 2006, then IBM Chairman and CEO Sam Palmisano said, "What is different now is that the concept of shareholders has expanded to stakeholders" (Blowfield and Googins 2006, p. 2). Thanks to social media and technological innovations, the stakeholder universe has expanded to a much wider set of individuals—both internal and external—that the enterprise must consider (Gitman and Enright 2015). Gitman and Enright, after a discussion with 16 member companies of Business for Social Responsibility (BSR), a global nonprofit organization, concluded, "In our increasingly transparent world, where a tweet can be as influential as an opinion in the board room, a company's strategy to engage with and learn from its stakeholders has never been more important, or complex" (Gitman and Enright 2015, p. 2).

The Boston College Center for Corporate Citizenship (2009) launched a report concluding a key competency of corporate leaders must be understanding stakeholders and their interests. According to the findings, "Nowadays, companies depend on favorable public opinion to ensure their license to enter, operate, and grow in markets around the world. This extends their agenda beyond compliance and following the law to understanding and engaging stakeholders and 'balancing' their interests in strategic decisions and operational practices" (p. 6).

The report also identified three reasons why the enterprise must be aware of the stakeholder landscapes where they do business:

1. Diverse stakeholders help shape the competitive context for business in a nation and globally;
2. They influence a firm's license to enter, grow and operate in local global markets; and therefore;
3. Understanding and monitoring the stakeholder landscape is essential to the long-term planning of an enterprise. (Boston College Center for Corporate Citizenship 2009, p. 5)

In one sense, this is not entirely new. After all, Arthur W. Page, who was vice president of public relations at AT&T from 1927 to 1946, said, "All business in a democratic society begins with public permission and exists by public approval" (http://awpagesociety.com/site/historical-perspective, n.d.). What is profoundly different today is the ability of stakeholders to get access to more information more quickly and easily and to share it with others instantly, potentially transforming public opinion about an enterprise and its operations virtually overnight.

Social Purpose and Corporate Character

The Arthur W. Page Society's 2012 report, *Building Belief: A New Model for Activating Corporate Character & Authentic Advocacy* (2012b, p. 7), posits that enterprises must adhere to a strong and admirable corporate character in order to earn stakeholder trust. Page defines corporate character as the unique, differentiating identity of the enterprise, as determined by its mission, purpose, values, culture, strategy, brand, and business model.

As the expectation increases that the enterprise must operate transparently and responsibly, while serving a social purpose, defining and aligning corporate character are critical.

In the 2016 *Edelman Trust Barometer*, 80 percent of respondents said they expect businesses can both increase profits and improve economic and social conditions in the communities in which they operate. It offered Tupperware as a prime example that has a global sales force in countries all over the world, including China, India, and Indonesia, where 3.1 million women can earn much-needed income to help drive sales revenue for the company. Additionally, it found that stakeholders respond positively to CEOs who can both earn profits and provide societal benefits; trust in CEOs has risen in the past five years.

Kanter (2011) noted that great companies extract more economic value by creating frameworks that "use societal value and human values as decision-making criteria" (p. 5) and meet stakeholder needs in a variety of ways. Social purpose and values are "at the core of an organization's identity" (p. 11). Therefore, seeking legitimacy or public approval by aligning enterprise objectives with social value is a business imperative. As Kanter (2011, p. 10) noted, "Only if leaders think of themselves as builders of social institutions can they master today's changes and challenges."

The Rise of Technology

Much of the change that is affecting the business environment is driven by technology. According to the International Data Corporation (2015), 3.2 billion people, or 44 percent of the world's population, now are connected on the Internet. This number is growing rapidly in every part of the world, driven by the explosion of mobile technology. Half of the world's population now has a mobile phone subscription, compared to just one in five 10 years ago (GSMA 2015).

The availability of inexpensive smartphones and laptops has made the Internet accessible to a whole new demographic. More than half of the population in each of the nations surveyed by the Pew Research Center (February 22, 2016) reported owning a mobile phone. The same study reported more than 9 in 10 own mobile phones in Jordan (95 percent), China (95 percent), Russia (94 percent), Chile (91 percent), and South

Africa (91 percent). The advent of tablets and smartwatches has also broadened the spectrum of Internet usage (Kah Leng 2016).

Each mobile device is not simply a receiver, but a potential global transmitter. For example, in sub-Saharan Africa, landline telephone penetration is near zero as the number of mobile devices has exploded, with many mobile owners using cell phones to take pictures/videos, send text messages, or do mobile banking (Pew Research Center 2015, April 15). Smartphones have helped reduce the number of people who do not have access to a bank account by 20 percent in the past three years (The World Bank 2014). As The World Bank noted, "As seen in sub-Saharan Africa, mobile money accounts can drive financial inclusion" (p. 3).

According to the IDC report, the mobile ecosystem is a tremendous economic driver; in 2014, the mobile industry accounted for 3.8 percent of global gross domestic product (GDP).

Software has had an impact on how businesses operate. In 2011, Andreessen contended that "software is eating the world," (p. 2) and software companies "are poised to take over large swathes of the economy" (p. 6). Four years later, Hendricks (2015, p. 1) wrote that now that software has eaten the world, it is starting to eat the company. In the same way that iPhones and iPads have turned into efficient ways to never need a personal assistant, Hendricks notes that software has slowly begun to make enterprises of all sizes leaner.

Innovation enabled by software is disrupting businesses of all sorts and transforming the economy. Google, Amazon, Uber, Airbnb, and others are transforming entire industries. In his 2015 book, Rise of the Robots: Technology and the Threat of a Jobless Future, Martin Ford, the founder of a Silicon Valley-based software firm, argues that "advancing information technology is pushing us toward a tipping point that is poised to ultimately make the entire economy less labor intensive" (p xvii).

A Deloitte study (2015b), on the other hand, concludes that "Machines will take on more repetitive and laborious tasks, but seem no closer to eliminating the need for human labor than at any time in the past 150 years." And in 2016, IBM CEO Ginni Rometty, in a letter to the U.S. President-elect Donald Trump, argued that there are many "new collar" jobs being created in technology that require training, but not a college degree (IBM 2016d).

Similarly, social media powered by technology have had a tremendous impact on business. In this smaller, flatter global world, social media have not only changed the way people access information and communicate with each other, but also created new communities of interest that exert powerful influence on existing and emerging institutions. Indeed, stakeholder groups have become more empowered, emboldened, and organized (Arthur W. Page Society 2016).

This speed of innovation correlates with technology's impact on society and people's behavior, and the speed with which it drives change. Despite several industry predictions that Moore's Law[4] is dying (Simonite May 13, 2016), researchers and companies like IBM and Google argue that the speed of innovation is not dying but taking a shift (*The Economist* 2016). This shift looks at innovation in terms of computing performance instead of transistor count.

Senior Vice President of Research and Marketing Intelligence of the Computing Technology Industry Association (CompTIA) Tim Hebert said, "Much of this growth [in the technology sector] can be attributed to the current trends in cloud computing, mobility, automation and social technologies that are reshaping businesses large and small (CompTIA 2016, p. 5)." The CompTIA's *Cyberstates 2016* report attributes 7.1 percent of the overall GDP to the U.S. tech industry. Other important factors are attributed to the growth of the "Internet of Things" (IoT), and the increased focus of cybersecurity.

Privacy and Cybersecurity

Businesses and governments have never been more reliant on technology and information sharing. Yet these same tools and interconnectedness make personal, business, and public property more vulnerable to attack than ever before.

In addition to traditional criminal networks and nonstate actors, state-sponsored cyber-attacks have become more frequent. According to the IBM *Cyber Security Index* (2016b), almost every industry saw

---

[4] Moore's Law posits that the number of transistors per square inch on integrated circuits, and consequently the processing power they produce, doubles every year.

an increase in security attacks in 2015, with companies experiencing a 64 percent increase in security incidents from 2014 to 2015; the most heavily hit industry was health care followed by manufacturing. The IBM *Cost of Data Breach Study* (2016a) found the average total cost of a data breach grew from $3.8 to $4 million. According to the Arthur W. Page Society (2016), "attacks target critical infrastructure systems, consumer data, business strategy and state secrets, creating new operational and reputational risks with which private and public sectors alike have struggled to keep up" (p. 8).

By 2018, more than half of all enterprises will use security service firms that specialize in data protection, security risk management, and security infrastructure management to enhance their security postures, with mobile security becoming a higher priority for consumers from 2017 onward (Gartner 2014). Morgan (2015) consolidated estimates by IT industry research and analyst firms to predict the *worldwide* cybersecurity market will grow from $75 billion in 2015 to $170 billion by 2020.

Societal Changes

Beyond these technological changes, there are also societal changes afoot in this new digital era that affect the way our stakeholders consume, interpret, and digest information. According to *The New CCO*, embracing diversity is a progressively important strategic imperative as business decisions and operations benefit from diversity of thought and inclusiveness.

Today, it seems the media news cycle is consumed by instances of intolerance of differences in communities across the world, which are being countered by greater efforts to drive toward equality in all societies. To be successful, the enterprise must understand and meet the needs of increasingly diverse internal and external stakeholders.

Diversity

Diversity is an important consideration for today's workforce and according to Deloitte (2014), it is not just visible aspects of diversity, but also diversity of thinking (more on this will be covered in Chapter 6). Diversity, then, is the measure and inclusion is the mechanism—both are needed to access top talent, drive performance and innovation, retain key employees, and understand companies. As the workforce is more multicultural than ever, a diverse workforce is not a program or marketing campaign, but "is a company's livelihood, and diverse perspectives and approaches are the only means of solving complex and challenging business issues" (Deloitte 2014, p. 92).

Age. The global workforce is becoming younger, older, and more urbanized (Deloitte 2014). The two greatest demographic trends that will impact the world in which we operate are the world's aging population and the rise of millennials (Pew Research Center 2009). The proportion of older adults in the labor force, referred to as the "grey ceiling," has been growing steadily over the past decades. In 2016, Millennials (ages 18 to 34 in 2015) surpassed the Baby Boomers (ages 51 to 69) (Fry 2016). Generation X (ages 35 to 50) is projected to pass the Boomers in population by 2028; until then, this demographic is projected to remain the "middle child" of generations—caught between two larger ones (Fry 2016). Research from the McKinsey Global Institute (2012) suggests that, by 2020, the world could have too few college-educated workers and that, in advanced economies, up to 95 million more low-skill workers than employers will be needed.

Gender. In business, the topic of gender equality continues to be an agenda item for most boardrooms. Women continue to participate in labor markets on an unequal basis compared to men. Gender differences in laws affect both developing and developed economies; almost 90 percent of 143 countries studied (UN Women 2015) have at least one legal difference restricting women's economic opportunities. Societal factors and more nuanced perceptions of gender also contribute to inequality in the workplace.

Despite women's gains, a large gender pay gap still exists. In 2013, women in the United States working full time, year round earned 78 percent of what men working equivalently earned (White House 2015). This number has been static for the past 15 years. The White House report on the gender pay gap suggests business and the economy can be improved, as well as worker productivity and retention, when workers are in jobs well suited to their skills and qualifications and policies ensure fair pay.

Lesbian, gay, bisexual, transgender, and queer (LGBTQ). The drive toward great equality in the LGBTQ community is also a major force within almost all cultures across the world. Nearly two dozen countries currently have national laws allowing gays and lesbians to marry, mostly in Europe and the Americas (Pew Research Center 2015, June). A meta-analysis of 36 research studies found that "less discrimination and more openness, in turn, are also linked to greater job commitment, improved workplace relationships, increased job satisfaction, improved health outcomes, and increased productivity among LGBT employees" (Badgett et al. 2013, p. 1).

Race. In the United States, Americans are more racially and ethnically diverse than in the past, and projected to be even more so in the coming decades (Cohn and Caumont 2016). However, there are challenges as companies and individuals are still battling racism. A recent Pew Research Center study (June 27, 2016) found two-thirds of black adults say blacks are treated less fairly than whites in the workplace. More than half of respondents to a 2015 survey (Pew Research Center 2015, August) reported racism is a "big problem" in today's society, and the United States needs to continue making changes to give blacks equal rights with whites. As enterprises become more global, more multiracial, and more multicultural, more are focusing on diversity and inclusion in the workplace, and tying compensation to recruitment and retention. The evidence is clear— diverse companies perform better (*Diversity Matters* 2015).

Religion. The religious profile of the world is rapidly changing, driven primarily by differences in fertility rates and the size of youth populations among the world's major religions, as well as by people switching faiths (Pew Research Center April 2, 2015). The Pew study predicted that by 2050:

- The number of Muslims will nearly equal the number of Christians around the world.
- In Europe, Muslims will make up 10 percent of the overall population.
- India will retain a Hindu majority but also will have the largest Muslim population of any country in the world, surpassing Indonesia.

- In the United States, Christians will decline from more than 75 percent of the population in 2010 to 67 percent in 2050, and Judaism will no longer be the largest non-Christian religion. Muslims will be more numerous in the United States, than people who identify as Jewish on the basis of religion.
- Four out of every 10 Christians in the world will live in sub-Saharan Africa. (2)

The most important finding of all is this:

Atheists, agnostics, and other people who do not affiliate with any religion—though increasing in countries such as the United States and France—will make up a declining share of the world's total population.

For those who see the divisiveness and violence attributed to religious clashes and conclude that secularism is the answer, the trends are not on their side. Yale University theologian Volf (2016) argues in *Flourishing: Why We Need Religion in a Globalized World* that "globalization and religions, as well as religions among themselves, need not clash violently but have internal resources to interact constructively and contribute to each other's betterment." As part of Princeton University's Faith and Work Initiative, research by Miller and Ewest (2010, p. 7) contended that understanding religious/spiritual identity at work can bring potential business benefits. These include "increased diversity and inclusion; avoidance of religious harassment or discrimination claims; respect for people of different faith traditions or worldviews, and possibly a positive impact on ethics programs, employee engagement, recruiting and retention."

Differing Value Systems

The rise of authoritarian capitalism, combined with gridlock and ineffectiveness in the Western democracies, is creating challenges for global business enterprises. Some believe state capitalism may be emerging as a preferred economic system in developing countries, based on the perceived success of that system in China. According to the Arthur W. Page

Society (2016), others believe that with economic progress will come more pressures for liberal democracy in China, Russia, the Middle East, and the developing world. Roughly 6 in 10 Chinese see growing international business ties as a way to improve local incomes (Pew Research Center 2014). Such sentiment may be rooted in China's recent experience. Wages have grown an average of more than 10 percent annually for more than a decade at a time when the country's merchandise exports were rising an average of 15 percent. In the Western democracies, political polarization and slow economic growth have combined to create voter disenchantment and disenfranchisement. This is driving a sentiment that globalization is not good for business. According to the Pew Research Center (2016, June 13), terrorist attacks, refugee crises, and economic decline are raising support for nationalism and focusing on their development rather than helping allies. The success of the Brexit vote in the United Kingdom and the Trump election in the United States both seemed motivated, at least in part, by concerns about job losses to and immigration from less-developed countries.

Health Care and the Environment

Three of the 17 sustainable goals outlined in the United Nations 2030 Agenda for Sustainable Development (2015) were health care, clean water and sanitation, and climate action. While the goals are fairly general, they are not mutually exclusive. A change in one, such as improving clean water, can have a dramatic impact on others like health care and the environment. The issues outlined by the UN should be considered by all enterprise CEOs in preparation for tomorrow's environment.

Health Care

In 2015, Deloitte released its *Global Health Outlook* report stating a "tug-of-war" exists between competing priorities of trying to meet the increasing demand for health care and reducing the rising costs (p. 1). Globalization is likely to bring issues as some countries struggle to ensure sufficient resources as developing markets are expanding, especially Asia and the Middle East. One given is that global health care spending will continue to increase. The enterprise needs to adapt to increased spending and changing health care needs. Businesses must contend with changes to health care policies and practices, including changes to government programs and movement toward consumer-driven health care. Radnofsky (2016) notes that 20 major enterprises (e.g., American Express, Macy's, and Verizon Communications) have allied to share information about members' employee health spending and outcomes. Down the road, they may form a purchasing group to negotiate lower prices.

Global health risks also impact businesses. According to the World Health Organization (2009), the leading global risks for mortality, responsible for 63 percent of all global deaths, are high blood pressure, tobacco use, high blood glucose, and physical inactivity (all noncommunicable diseases or NCDs). Five leading risk factors (childhood underweight, unsafe sex, alcohol use, unsafe water sanitation, and high blood pressure) are responsible for one-fourth of all global deaths. According to the Harvard School of Public Health and World Economic Forum (September 2011), over the next 20 years, NCDs will cost more than US$30 trillion, representing 48 percent of global GDP in 2010, and push millions of people below the poverty line. Nearly half of all business leaders surveyed worry at least one NCD will hurt their company's bottom line in the next five years and the enterprise is a key change agent facilitating the adoption of healthier lifestyles, issues that cause "decreased productivity in the workplace, prolonged disability, and diminished resources within families" (p. 5).

Clean Water

In 2010, the UN General Assembly passed a resolution that clean drinking water and sanitation "are essential to the realization of all human rights" (UNDESA 2015, p. 1), specifically water that is "sufficient, safe, accessible, physically accessible, and affordable" (UNDESA 2015, p. 4). According to Mekonnen and Hoekstra (2016), two-thirds of the world's population lives under conditions of "severe" water scarcity at least one month of the year, with nearly half living in Asia. Even though the 2015 *Global Risks Report* by the World Economic Forum (WEF) ranked water crisis as one of the three highest concerns to society worldwide, a WEF survey of executives found water only ranked 13th. According to members of the 2030 Water Resources Group (2009), water issues will affect nearly every business sector. In the *CEO Water Mandate*, the UN Global Compact (2016) identified three water risks (see Figure 1.1): physical, reputational, and regulatory. Physical risks can occur by having too much water, not enough water for production or processing, or water that is unfit for use. Water scarcity can also impact energy and food production, not to mention increase costs; however, more companies are implementing water reduction policies. Companies can also be affected by reputational risks as stakeholders are demanding companies be responsible and sustainable. Regulatory risks can occur when infrastructure or the lack of water quality regulations have an effect on the costs to do business as water sources must be cleaned prior to use.

An important factor in clean water is its cost and economic impact. The World Health Organization (2016) found achieving the goal for halving the proportion of people without sustainable access to both improved water supply and sanitation would give a triple return on investment. Poor water policies, lack of oversight, increased water demand, increased urbanization, lack of funding, inconsistent water policies across countries, and lack of stakeholder involvement (2030 Water Resources Group 2009) are some of the identified water challenges of the future. Many enterprises

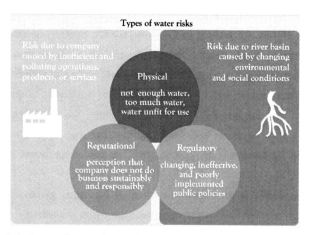

Figure 1.1 Interrelationships of types of water risks

Source: UN Global Compact: http://ceowatermandate.org/why-stewardship/stewardship-is-good-for-business/

are affected by water shortages or the potential for water scarcity. One example of this is SABMiller, the world's second-largest brewer measured by revenue, which enacted measures beyond simply reducing water use to focus on long-term water use (3p Contributor 2015). In 2004, Pepsi Bottling and Coca-Cola closed down plants in India that local farmers believed were in competition for water (2030 Water Resources Group 2009). McKinsey & Company, a member of the 2030 Water Resources Group, predicted that water would be a strategic factor for most companies noting, "All businesses will need to conserve, and many will make a market in conservation. Tomorrow's leaders in water productivity are getting into position today" (p. 31).

Climate Change

In a PwC 2014 survey, 46 percent of CEOs agreed that resource scarcity and climate change will transform the enterprise the most over the next five years, especially dealing with a rise in energy prices (despite a time when fossil fuel prices are low) and increasing government regulation. According to the *Climate Vulnerability Monitor*, losses attributed to climate change are predicted to increase rapidly with an estimated 3.2 percent of GDP in net average global losses by 2030 (Fundacion DARA Internacional 2012). In 2012, PwC released a climate change report suggesting radical enterprise action is needed to plan for a warming world (Confino 2012). According to Confino, CEOs need to be prepared to tackle climate change issues: "Sectors dependent on food, water, energy or ecosystem services need to scrutinize the resilience and viability of their supply. More carbon-intensive sectors need to anticipate more invasive regulation and the possibility of stranded assets" (p. 12). Siegel (2013) maintains that "without a doubt" the number one impact of climate change on business will be "uncertainty," as this area's future is hard to predict (p. 7).

Sustainability is an important force of business, as consumers are increasingly demanding enterprises become more sustainable. The UN Global Compact (Accenture CEO Study 2013) found that 93 percent of CEOs believe that sustainability will be important to the future success of their business, but only 34 percent report making sufficient efforts to address *global* sustainability challenges. The key, though, lies in the hands of the consumer. While the report found investors will not be the ones pressuring growth, more than half of respondents said the customer is key to influencing the approach, and 87 percent said the reputation of sustainability is important in consumer purchasing decisions. A McKinsey & Company (2014) study reported reputation management related to sustainability is a challenge because, while reputation management is a top reason for enterprises to address sustainability, many are not pursuing these value-added types of reputation-building activities. Further, they note that the most effective sustainability programs are building in strong performance processes, aggressive internal and external goals, a focused strategy, and leadership buy-in.

Summary

With the dramatic changes in society in this digital age and for the future, understanding the interwoven factors that impact society is critical. Technology will continue to grow and change as innovations become more diffused through society, and processors and equipment become faster, smaller, and cheaper. More community-driven initiatives, and the proliferation of social media platforms, demonstrate that power has shifted to the stakeholder. With the influx and success of start-ups, traditional business models are changing. Society is changing dramatically and, as people are moving, shifting, and ideologies are melding, understanding and anticipating needs will be key to enterprise success. Ensuring fairness and a diverse and inclusive (D&I) workforce will be critical. The environment will play a starring role as the enterprise needs to think about how costs and demands for sustainability will impact the future. With all these changes, the role of the CCO has never been as important as it is today. The Arthur W. Page Society report, *The New CCO: Transforming Enterprises in a Changing World* (2016), describes the need for effective communication today and for the future. The CCO must be an *integrator*, a *builder* of digital engagement systems, and a *strategic leader* and *counselor*. With these changing times, it is certain that change is inevitable. Choosing to ignore change is not an option.

CHAPTER 2

The Evolving Corporate Communication Function

Paul Argenti, Maril MacDonald, and Sean O'Neill

As the role of the chief communication officer (CCO) evolves, it is important to understand her unique strategic contribution to the operation of the enterprise. Over the last few decades, a profound shift has occurred in how leaders view the communication function within organizations, from a tactical and superficial focus to a more strategic and elevated perspective. As a result, it has evolved to enjoy more responsibility, importance, and impact than ever before.

Multilateral demands from a range of constituencies, declining confidence in business, and the impacts of globalization are all propelling strategic communication to the center of modern enterprise management, and enterprises are reacting by revising budgets and internal structure to support the function. This chapter explores the evolving CCO role, the growing mandate and responsibilities of the function, the increased focus on integration and collaboration, and the effect of an increasingly globalized, interconnected business landscape.

The Emergence of Corporate Communication

Early in the 20th century, as big business became more of a force in society, increased demands for transparency from a variety of internal and external constituencies and changes in laws and regulations ushered in the emergence of a new corporate function: public relations. Whether they wanted to or not, enterprises had to respond to constituencies at an unprecedented rate and volume. Managers realized that they would need to dedicate resources to manage the near constant flow of information.

The first senior corporate public relations executive who was more than just a publicity man was Arthur W. Page, who served as vice president, public relations, for AT&T from 1927 to 1946. Page was already a well-respected national business magazine editor and columnist when he was hired by AT&T. Page Society founder Ed Block explained in 1993,

> When he was offered the job, [Page] told the chief executive that he would take it only if it was a policy making position. Corporate policy. Not "communications" policy. He understood clearly from the outset that good public relations is a product of wise and timely policy.

Page also understood that good public relations was essential to the survival of business. "All business in a democratic society begins with public permission and exists by public approval," he said. He also believed that good public relations flowed from the authentic reality of the company's actions. "Public relations is 90 percent doing and 10 percent talking about it," Page famously said (Arthur W. Page Society n.d.).

Another early pioneer was Paul Garrett, who joined General Motors in a similar position in 1936. Like Page, Garrett believed public relations was integral to company policy and argued that it was the responsibility of everyone in the organization (Henige 1995).

From its founding in 1983, the Page Society aspired to this kind of elevated, policy-making role for its members, who primarily are CCOs and public relations agency CEOs. As the role of corporate public relations evolved, some professionals like Larry Foster at Johnson & Johnson, and advisers, like Harold Burson, founder of Burson Marsteller, did have full access to CEOs and were involved in enterprise policy decisions. Foster, for example, was a chief adviser to J&J Chairman Jim Burke during the Tylenol crisis in 1982, which is widely seen as a model of corporate crisis management (New York Times October 30, 2013).

In many other enterprises, though, corporate communication became a decentralized function, with employee communication often located in human resources, investor relations in finance, customer relations in marketing, and media relations in public relations, which often did not report to the CEO (Argenti 2016, pp. vi–vii). Thus, the importance of the Page Society's mission: "To strengthen the enterprise leadership role of the chief communications officer"—a phrase that suggests that the leadership role of many CCOs is not as strong as it could be (Arthur W. Page Society n.d.).

In *The Authentic Enterprise* (Arthur W. Page Society 2007), the Page Society observed that for many years, the enterprise communication function simply served as a liaison of the enterprise and was responsible for developing and maintaining media relationships, corporate journalism, internal events, and speechwriting. The goal was information, and the measurement of value was activity-based (volume of press coverage, readership of company publications).

The financial scandals of WorldCom and Enron in the early 2000s drove changes in public expectations of business to be more authentic, responsive, and responsible (Argenti 2016). This trend was not isolated to the United States. Massive accounting scandals at the Netherlands' Royal Ahold and at Italian dairy-foods firm Parmalat—sometimes referred to as "Europe's Enron"—dominated headlines in the same period. These scandals alarmed the public about the lack of transparency in business and the concept of reputation evolved from a communication-led theory to a strategy-based enterprise necessity.

The Authentic Enterprise (Arthur W. Page Society 2007) reported that by 2007 the role of corporate communication had evolved to be a strategic planner of enterprise positioning, focused on driving coverage, influencing external criteria, changing culture, and influencing strategy and policy—a role more like that assumed by Page and Garrett in earlier times. The goal was to influence brand perceptions and enterprise reputation, and the measurement of value was attitude-based (assessing corporate reputation and employee commitment). The CEOs who were surveyed as a part of that report saw the role of corporate communication evolving from reactive to proactive to interactive:

- Reactive communications exhibit the traditional role of playing defense—protecting the company's reputation and responding effectively to crises and other unexpected developments.

- Proactive communications involve the more advanced skills required to play offense—seeking new opportunities to enhance the company's reputation.
- Interactive communications represent the future of the profession—the emerging imperative to build values-based relations and two-way collaboration with diverse constituencies. (p. 40)

The Growing Mandate

CEOs now regard the communications function as highly strategic, particularly in light of heightened demands for transparency and corporate purpose (Arthur W. Page Society May, 2017).

> Across the board, the CEOs regarded reactive approaches as inadequate, the report stated. "Even the proactive approaches that have strengthened during the past couple of decades, while valuable, are no longer sufficient. ... CEOs acknowledge that these new forms of interactive communications are in an early, largely aspirational stage today. But they expect their chief communications officer to take on this new responsibility." (p. 17)

In the ensuing decade, the evolving business environment and stakeholder expectations, described in Chapter 1, have accelerated demands on the CCO and the enterprise communication function. Most important, the CCO role is transitioning from functional expert to business leader. CCOs must, therefore, be able to deliver effective strategic communication and, at the same time, contribute to high-level corporate decision making. A 2015 Korn Ferry Institute survey of Fortune 500 companies examining the evolving role of the CCO found that "nearly all respondents (more than 91 percent) identified 'providing leadership on reputation, values, and culture' across the enterprise" as receiving more attention and effort today (Korn Ferry 2015, p. 14).

As the enterprise's shepherd of authenticity and reputation, CCOs increasingly are focused on how a company's actions and behaviors affect the perceptions of its key constituencies, just as Page and Garrett were in an earlier era. The Page Society introduced a report in 2012 outlining the "Page Model of Enterprise Communication," which holds that the first responsibility of the CCO is to help create a strong corporate character. Explored in more detail in Chapter 4, corporate character is the source of the enterprise's unique, differentiating identity, consisting of purpose, mission, values, culture, business model, and strategy. The idea is that, to be trusted by stakeholders, an enterprise must define and activate a corporate character that is worthy of trust (Arthur W. Page Society 2012a).

Developing a "One-Company culture" (Argenti March 2016, p.15) is a strategic imperative focusing on corporate character (Chapter 4 will examine this in detail). The results of implementing such a culture are a clearer corporate vision and a guiding principle for executing strategy through communication. The Institute for Public Relations recently concluded from a comprehensive study, "By aiding employees in drawing a line-of-sight between their individual jobs and the marketplace, against the backdrop of the company's strategy, businesses can achieve Organizational Clarity and, ultimately, organizational success" (Institute for Public Relations 2016, p. 6).

Having a strategy and communicating it so that everyone can act on it is a critical first step. The strategy must be clear and understandable, it must be true, and most important of all it must be consistent (Argenti and van Riel n.d.). A One-Company culture involves deep employee engagement, an entrepreneurial spirit across all enterprise levels, and authentic relationships between managers and employees to align them around a strategic road map to harness maximum individual and collective brainpower and keep the enterprise nimble and responsive to the world evolving around it. The growth of large enterprises over the last century has led to incredible progress and opportunity. That growth, however, has also created organizational complexity. The idea of thousands of people operating as one is next to impossible without a concerted effort by a senior management team focused on strategy, execution through communication, and culture.

The enterprise needs to find ways to translate its vision into a handful of words capturing the imagination of employees all over the world. Orit Gadiesh, chairman of consulting firm Bain & Company, wrote an article for *Harvard Business Review* in 2001 (with James L. Gilbert) entitled "Transforming Corner-Office Strategy into Frontline Action" that focused on how to distill "their strategy into a phrase and have it used to drive consistent strategic action throughout their organizations" (p. 74). Earlier, she used Dell's "Be direct" and GE's "Be number one or number two in every industry in which we compete or get out" as some of the best examples of this vision distillation (Gadiesh and Gilbert 2001).

Today, we might look at Walmart's "Save Money, Live Better" as perhaps the best example of enterprise strategy distilled into a few words. The dual focus on value through low prices and values through sustainability and responsible business behavior has transformed the largest corporation in the world (by revenue) in terms of its relationships with suppliers and its willingness to focus on major societal issues within and outside the corporation (Argenti 2016).

Even the most authentic and illuminating codes of conduct and values, however, do not automatically result in supportive behavior throughout an entire employee base. Most critical is management's maintenance of a strong two-way dialogue about the company's direction and strategy with employees, including a concrete action plan for how people at all enterprise levels can support it through their individual roles. Once employees become part of the dialogue, and understand their personal connection with corporate strategy and values, they are more likely to believe their best interest is to further the best interests of the organization as well. That critical connection when employee self-interest and corporate self-interest fuse is the cornerstone of a One-Company culture (Argenti and Van Riel 2016).

In addition to culture and values, corporate character includes a sense of purpose with a focus on creating value, not just for customers and shareholders, but for all stakeholders and society in general. There is a growing emphasis on corporate responsibility,[1] which continues to grow in importance as companies are expected to do more than just give back to the community. Companies must ensure they have a clear set of operating principles and definitions of responsible behavior. A clear example is provided by Starbucks, a company that thrives in striking a balance between marketplace performance and social impact. Corey duBrowa, former

---

[1] Initially defined as corporate *social* responsibility (CSR), the phrase has been redefined as corporate responsibility (CR) to note that responsibility is more than merely social in nature and often to remove the company from being identified.

Starbucks senior vice president of global communications, explains, "Collaborating with marketing and category leadership ensures that the Starbucks brand and approach presents an integrated view of the company as one capable of leading marketplace performance while executing its business through the lens of humanity" (Arthur W. Page Society 2016, p. 27). The CCO is often looked to for guidance in building these principles, a process that requires input and buy-in across the entire enterprise.

Modern businesses are battling to build and maintain strong identities and global reputations, and today's CCO serves as a "conscience counselor" to ensure the honesty and authenticity of an enterprise's rhetoric, values, and the responsibility of its behavior with the interests of all constituencies in mind (Arthur W. Page Society 2016).

The second role of the CCO in the Page Model is to build stakeholder advocacy, explored in more detail in Chapter 5. This overarching responsibility requires CCOs to build relationships across a greater number of constituents, internally and externally, to ensure symmetrical engagement and dialogue—not just one-way communication from the enterprise (Grunig 1987; Korn Ferry Institute 2012). As the shepherd of enterprise positioning, reputation, and authenticity, the modern CCO is responsible for creating and influencing an ecosystem of stakeholders and advocates; stewarding the company's values, brand, and reputation; shaping the culture and behaviors; creating the new, blended physical/virtual work environment; and empowering employees as communicators (Arthur W. Page Society 2016). As a result, today's most forward-thinking CEOs are looking for CCOs to take a more strategic and interactive role within senior leadership.

In an increasingly transparent world, an enterprise can no longer be different things to different constituencies; it must be one thing across its entire ecosystem. CCOs must assert leadership in building and managing multistakeholder relationships. Additionally, the communication function serves to build support among multiple constituencies and civil society (Arthur W. Page Society 2007). In other words, the CCO ensures responsiveness to all stakeholders—internal and external, financial and customers, employees and management.

These new roles for the CCO and the corporate communication function require new skills and capabilities, a topic that will be examined more closely in Chapter 9. As a result, CCOs are frequently functioning as an attractor, builder, and distributor of talent. The CCO's ability,

To cultivate and disseminate talent strategically, in ways that fully leverage the collective capabilities of the communications [*sic*] function, address core business needs and further organizational goals, is an emerging expectation of the CCO that has become even more critical given the dynamic environment in which we now operate. (Arthur W. Page Society 2016, p. 16)

As the scope of responsibilities continues to grow, there is an increasing mandate for communication executives to serve as high-level, strategic advisers to CEOs and senior leadership teams. In a report based on interviews with CEOs in 2013, the Page Society reported that more CCOs report directly to their CEO than they did in 2007, and more are on their company's executive committee, where most major strategic decisions are made, especially at many larger companies.

Today's enterprises require a CCO who is an informed, vocal, compelling, and trusted counselor to the firm's leadership. The communication function is relied upon to identify, interpret, and act upon changes in the external environment; stay ahead of events by monitoring traditional and social media; engage with regulators, policy makers, intergovernmental organizations (IGOs), and nongovernmental organizations (NGOs); and build trusting and lasting relationships with constituencies. This requires business acumen and "a deep understanding of the company and the industry as a crucial source of credibility inside the C-Suite," according to the CEOs interviewed by Page (Arthur W. Page Society 2016, p. 13). Gary Sheffer, former vice president of strategic communications at General Electric, explains that "the diversity of issues that today's CCOs are expected to help lead is greater than ever. This requires CCOs to have a broader lens and more depth on the issues that can affect the success of the company" (Arthur W. Page Society 2016, p. 21). As Mike Fernandez, former corporate vice president for corporate affairs at Cargill, put it: "We talk about engaging and positively shaping the environment in which the company operates. That has moved the function from being not just a group of communicators, but of business strategists and problem solvers" (Arthur W. Page Society 2016, p. 24).

The Increased Focus on Integration and Collaboration

When it comes to structuring communication activities within the enterprise, challenges still persist. One challenge is how to maintain *consistency* in enterprise corporate communication while maintaining a level of flexibility across business units. While centralizing communication under one senior officer at global, national, or regional headquarters provides the easiest way for enterprises to achieve that consistency, that amount of control can adversely affect the creativity and productivity of the enterprise. The effective balance often depends on enterprise size, the geographic dispersion of its offices, and the diversity of its products and services. For an enterprise like General Electric, for example, there is simply no way that such a large and diversified enterprise could remain completely centralized in all of its communication activities. The same might not be said about a smaller and functionally focused enterprise, such as Chipotle. Further, because the new roles of the corporate communication function are to build corporate character and stakeholder advocacy, and because effectively doing that requires the commitment of the entire enterprise, there is a growing imperative for the CCO to work collaboratively across the enterprise. This will be explored in detail in Chapter 7.

The core objective of the modern communication function is to build reputation, which is a prerequisite for business success. This cannot be achieved without taking an *outside-in approach*, thinking and acting holistically. Today's constituencies are both interconnected and interdependent, and the benefits of having *integrated teams* and programming are impossible to ignore. Integration is increasingly important as enterprises become more international and as more business is conducted remotely. With this level of dispersion, it is vital that employees be on the same page regarding company goals, mission, vision, values, and priorities. CCOs are embracing and driving cross-functional collaboration and partnerships, both within the enterprise and across the C-Suite. They are working more closely with other C-Suite functions, especially the chief human resources officer, chief marketing officer, and chief information officer. According to the Page Jam (an online discussion that garnered the opinions of Page members), CCOs say their collaboration with C-Suite colleagues is up 32 percent from five years ago (Arthur W. Page Society 2016). Engagement increased most with the Chief Information Officer (CIO) (a 42 percent increase from five years ago). This illustrated how CCOs are increasingly leveraging digital and mobile platforms to engage key stakeholders (Arthur W. Page Society 2016). Whether collaborating with the Chief Human Resources Officer (CHRO) on employee engagement and corporate character, with the CIO on developing a more robust data analytics capability, or with the CMO on aligning brand and customer engagement with that of other stakeholders, greater integration and collaboration support more strategically successful communications efforts across the firm. This collaboration should be supported through innovative approaches to re-engineer the concept of teams and facilitate greater cross-functional integration and collaboration (Arthur W. Page Society 2016).

At the firms that best understand the value and importance of the CCO function, CCOs enjoy direct reporting relationships to the CEO. GE's iconic former CEO Jack Welch explained in the 2016 Page Society report, "The CEO and the CCO have a unique relationship; total trust, very intimate, in it together, buy-in on the mission…their relationship is closer to the CCO than any other person on the staff, and as a result they know more about what's going on." Communication executives act as reputation stewards in a highly interconnected landscape, leading integrated initiatives across teams, and building platforms and processes to effectively engage with the world (Arthur W. Page Society 2016). Everyone across the organization, from the top down, participates in shaping and preserving that reputation. The CCO is ideally situated to work across the C-Suite to ensure that corporate character is reflected across functions, that values are being practiced, and so on. Maintaining the trust of the public—the social license to operate—depends on making sure that the entire organization is aligned around character, culture, values, purpose, and so forth.

Integration of communication activities across the business remains a pressing challenge. The 2015 Brands2Life/PR Week Annual Communication Directors survey found that 73 of the 100 communication directors surveyed put integration at the top of their to-do list. Most CCOs believe that whatever formal structure is applied within an enterprise, the future will require more *ad hoc*, fluid approaches requiring coordination, collaboration, and strategic integration skills. Whatever structural approach an organization chooses, research from the Page Society suggests that:

- The CCO must have a direct working relationship with the CEO and C-Suite colleagues;
- All C-Suite members must collaborate on both activating corporate character and engaging constituencies around it; and
- The CCO should have responsibility for systematically managing enterprise stakeholder engagement through social media and other means. (Arthur W. Page Society 2016, p. 6)

Integration and collaboration are not only internal prerequisites. The communication function must be able to integrate strategic communication across multiple external stakeholder constituencies to achieve a single end. CCOs are supplementing in-house capabilities with external expertise in areas like behavioral economics, data analytics, and content creation while forging new partnerships with NGOs that allow them to better navigate rapidly changing social and environmental challenges (Arthur W. Page Society 2016).

The Road Ahead

The pace of this change is only going to increase, and with it the role of CCO will continue to broaden and diversify. The modern communication function is responsible for understanding the wide range of stakeholder constituencies and navigating an increasingly complex environment. Success will come through the development of increasingly sophisticated Digital Engagement Systems that map stakeholders, engender understanding of them (usually through data), and systematize the process of engaging with them, not merely as segments but as individuals. In form, these systems would resemble the digital commerce systems through which companies are leveraging data about online behavior to discern individual stakeholder wants and needs and cater to them more effectively (Arthur W. Page Society March 2016, p. 32).

Building these new systems, described in more detail in Chapter 8, will require entirely new skills and capabilities. As the evolution of the role of the CCO continues, there will remain a need for a strong CCO who intimately understands the inner workings of the enterprise and the forces affecting it, the diverse stakeholder constituencies affected by it and how to build relationships with them, and the dynamics of earning and maintaining the public's trust (Arthur W. Page Society 2016). Additionally, according to the 2016 Global Communication Report (Holmes 2016), corporate communication executives around the world believe that, over the next five years, both they and their public relations agency partners will be expected to deliver more strategy, content, channels, creativity, and measurement.

As the world continues to globalize, the CCO will increasingly be required to interpret and plan for the impact that macro/socioeconomic and geopolitical events will have on the enterprise. This means that CCOs must have a global perspective and strategic mindset to effectively communicate across cultures and understand the complexities of managing communication for global enterprises. CCOs must possess the ability to strategize multicultural communication within and across enterprises and integrate innovative global communication strategies. Additionally, CCOs are increasingly required to manage global teams of communicators to ensure consistent, integrated, and effective messaging across oceans.

The requirements for success continue to increase. There is growing emphasis on international experience, cross-cultural management, and language skills. In an increasingly globalized world, fueled by the ubiquity of the Internet and 24-hour news cycle, corporate reputation can be destroyed in seconds. As modern business continues to learn about the immense value of using communication to execute strategy most effectively, the CCO role will become even more critical to the success of the enterprise in the 21st century (Arthur W. Page Society 2016).

Case: Defining and Supporting Enterprise Strategy Through Stakeholder Partnership

A Company Transformed and Challenged

Established in 1864 by Gerard Adriaan Heineken in Amsterdam, the Netherlands, HEINEKEN is the world's most international brewer and the leading developer and marketer of premium beer and cider brands. Led by the Heineken® brand, the Group has a powerful portfolio of more than 250 international, regional, local, and specialty beers and ciders. The company employs nearly 85,000 people and operates 160 breweries in 70 countries.

Over the last 15 years, the company has transformed its geographic footprint from being a predominantly European and mature market business to a business that now derives two-thirds of its volumes and profits from emerging markets in Africa, Asia, and Latin America. Today, HEINEKEN is the number one brewer in Europe and the number three brewer by volume in the world.

In 2014, HEINEKEN launched its "Greenprint" strategy, mapping out what it saw as the keys to future growth. For the first time, sustainability in the form of its "Brewing a Better World" (BaBW) approach was included as one of the company's six strategic global pillars. The six key BaBW focus areas were agreed upon with the company's stakeholders and covered the key material impacts across the business operations: water, CO_2 reduction, responsible consumption, sustainable sourcing, health and safety, and communities.

Challenge and Opportunity in Equal Measure

In the confluence of the new strategy, the company's transformed global footprint and macro issues, the corporate relations (CR) function led by Chief Corporate Relations Officer (CCRO) Sean O'Neill saw challenges. If the new strategic pillars were not executed with a clear understanding of external context and stakeholder concerns they could fail to deliver growth and damage hard-won reputation. Given the integration of sustainability within the strategy, it would be challenging, particularly in developing markets, to ensure the delivery of *inclusive* growth that would benefit all stakeholders and communities.

The CR function within HEINEKEN spans public and government affairs, public policy, sustainable development external communication, employee communication, and brand/consumer PR. Programming across key stakeholders is integrated across these disciplines to ensure a consistency of message, delivery, and approach and also to increase influence and impact. At global, regional, and in most of the operating companies, the most senior functional leader is a member of the executive management team and has the remit and responsibility to act as a business leader and functional expert.

Input, Integration, and Alignment

Externally, the function led conversations with key stakeholders centered on materiality, desired outcomes, and quantifying the trends. Internally, a series of facilitated discussions at local, regional, and global levels engaged cross-functional team members essential to building the new approach.

A number of key areas for potential partnerships were identified including human rights in emerging markets, the water/food/energy nexus particularly in water- and food-scarce areas, diversity and inclusion, biodiversity and animal rights and welfare. Following presentations at both the company's Corporate Affairs Committee and global Executive Team the outline strategy was confirmed.

"Proof of Concept"—The First Partnership Forcing Positive Change

It was proposed that the first partnership would address the challenge of the water/food/energy nexus. By 2030, the world is expected to require 40 percent more water and 50 percent more energy. Population growth, changing lifestyles, and climate change will place increasing pressure on the environment, particularly on water, energy, and food. As a brewer, HEINEKEN touches all three of these areas. While it was felt that the company had made good progress on the individual elements of local sourcing, water footprint, and energy/CO_2 reduction plans, a strong partnership in Africa would allow the company to build a more inclusive and integrated approach.

The company reviewed several possible partnership options before approaching UNIDO, the United Nations Industrial Development Organization, a specialized agency of the UN with primary responsibility for promoting industrial development in developing countries and in countries with economies in transition. It had significant experience of working with private sector companies and governments to address exactly the issues on which HEINEKEN was seeking to partner.

Discussions and negotiations with UNIDO were led by Michael Dickstein, global director sustainable development, and Patrick Villemin, regional CR director Africa Middle East. Both understood the importance of getting the first partnership right and ensured that objectives and expectations were clear. In March 2015, the formal partnership agreement with UNIDO was signed at their Vienna Headquarters.

The ongoing partnership focuses mainly on water stewardship initiatives in "water-scarce" areas. The initiatives developed by the partnership directly support HEINEKEN in its commitment to reduce water consumption to 3.3 hectoliters (1 hl = 100 liters) of water per hectoliter of beer brewed in its breweries in Algeria, Egypt, Ethiopia, Indonesia, Mexico, Nigeria, and Tunisia. Two multistakeholder workshops have been held in Ethiopia and Nigeria on the future of local watersheds.

The partnership is also focused on efforts to improve the livelihoods of local communities, as well as reducing fossil-fuel dependency at Heineken's developing country breweries and supplying excess clean energy back to local communities. The company continues to establish new partnerships that are resulting in senior-level conversations that build understanding of the noncommercial issues and risks that the company faces across its operating footprint. As a result, the company will be better prepared and positive impact will be more widely felt across stakeholders when appropriate change is made.

Key Learnings

1. *CCOs must address strategic challenges from an enterprisewide perspective.* It is critical to anticipate conflicts between enterprise strategy and societal trends/norms.

2. *A clear, strategic, agreed-upon role for communication/corporate affairs is critical.* This gives the function the mandate to influence, challenge, and advise on strategy and decision making.
3. *Know what you are getting into.* Partnerships require commitment. The recommendations for change—if sufficiently powerful—will require financial investment and behavioral change.

Summary

In an interconnected world, the ability of enterprises to build and protect brand and reputation requires development of a strong corporate character and authentic stakeholder engagement. Increasingly, enterprises are turning to the CCO for leadership. The CCO needs a seat at the C-Suite table when strategic decisions are being made, because corporate communication is part of a fully aligned strategy. Few other executives have the broad and deep understanding across stakeholder constituencies that is required to make the complex and mission-critical decisions facing today's enterprises. Smart CEOs and managers will learn that prioritizing communication will allow them to build an integrated culture and a reputation with constituents, and to execute strategy more effectively; those who ignore this imperative do so at their peril.

CHAPTER 3

The Trust Imperative

**Richard Edelman, Stephen A. Greyser,
E. Bruce Harrison, and Tom Martin**

Trust: It is one of the earliest feelings human beings have. Small children place their complete trust in parents, for their care, nourishment, safety, and well-being. As they grow older and wiser they make choices about whom to trust, and whom not to trust. This is true of people, and it is true of the enterprises they build.

Trust is not something that can be claimed, by individuals or by organizations; instead it must be *earned*. Enterprises—businesses, governments, nonprofits, labor unions, sports teams, and membership organizations—all learn through experience that their stakeholders judge them more by their actions and behavior than by their words.

Despite this reality, enterprises and the individuals who lead them continue to betray the trust placed in them through decisions that in hindsight seem hard to understand. Consider these examples:

- Volkswagen admitted in 2016 that it had systematically designed its diesel cars to evade emissions tests. In the months following this shocking revelation, the CEO of the global company resigned in disgrace, sales plummeted, and the company is now preparing to pay billions of dollars to the customers who were deceived.
- Valeant Pharmaceuticals was accused of targeting acquisition candidates that made drugs considered essential to patients with life-threatening illnesses. Once the companies were acquired, Valeant imposed exorbitant price increases on these medicines, leaving patients and their insurers with no option but to pay the higher prices.

- Toshiba overstated its profits by $1.2 billion between 2008 and 2014, largely by understating its costs on long-term projects. Two of its former CEOs were accused of putting intense pressure on subordinates to meet internal profit goals following the 2008 recession. Though both stepped down, they continued to receive payments from the company.

Hardly a week goes by without another example of misdeeds that further damage trust in organizations. Successful leaders in enterprises large and small pay close attention to building authenticity and stakeholder trust.

Accounting for Trust: The Edelman Trust Barometer

Edelman (2016), one of the largest global communication firms, publishes an annual *Trust Barometer* that is presented annually at the World Economic Forum in Davos, Switzerland. The 2016 report showed that large corporations are still facing major barriers in restoring trust with customers and communities. Government institutions and the media fared even worse. Only 53 percent of the general public expressed trust in business, while only 49 percent trusted the media and just 43 percent trusted government institutions.

The 2016 vote by Great Britain to leave the European Union and the election of Donald Trump as president in the United States represented further confirmation of the collapse of trust in the institutions of business, government, and media. This rejection of the establishment is the culmination of a gradual estrangement of mass population from elites since the Great Recession of 2008, as seen in the 2016 *Edelman Trust Barometer*, with the United States and United Kingdom as the poster children of the trust divide.

The average gap in trust in the enterprise between the elite and mass populations has grown to 12 points (across the developing and developed world). In the United States the difference is 19 points; in the United Kingdom it is 17 points; and in India it is 16 points. The *Edelman Trust Barometer* revealed that trust inequality correlates with income inequality across the world. In 18 of 28 countries surveyed, Edelman saw a double-digit gap in trust between high-income and low-income respondents. In the United States, the gap is 31 points, in France it is 29 points, in Brazil it is 26 points, and in India it is 22 points. The 2016 trust divide also corresponds to the public's expectations of its future well-being. For example, in two-thirds of the countries surveyed, fewer than half of mass population respondents think they will be better off in five years.

The rapid pace of innovation amplifies uncertainty in business. "Unicorn" companies (defined as any tech startup company that reaches a $1 billion market value as determined by private or public investment) continue to disrupt long-time leaders in travel, consumer products, and food, with new services offering transparent consumer feedback. Globalization has prompted relocation of factories and compression of wages, even while pressing to deliver a vast array of goods at affordable prices. The relentless pursuit of efficiency is rewarded by short-term demands of financial markets. Stakeholders appear to grow more skeptical as access to information becomes easier. More than half of respondents in the *Trust Barometer* study found the change of pace in marketing too rapid, with the instances of false claims increasing. Trust is shaped by access to accurate, valid, and reliable data. Stakeholders now form belief, the *Trust Barometer* indicates, through personal or online conversations; Edelman (2016) suggests that consumers must see, hear, or read a story in five *different* places before lasting opinions are formed about a product, candidate, or other entity.

There is a dispersion of authority away from CEOs and government leaders, who are now regarded as only half as credible as "a person like me or a fellow employee." It is not surprising then that 47 percent of respondents surveyed in the *Trust Barometer* said that they could not name a single enterprise CEO. What's more, while most CEOs believe that their duty is to center their communication on the operational and financial aspects of their enterprise, 80 percent of those surveyed in 2016 said that a CEO should be personally visible in discussing societal issues like income inequality, a finding echoed by the Arthur W. Page Society (2017).

Stakeholders in enterprises respond positively to CEOs who believe they can fulfill the dual mandate of earning profits and providing societal benefits. Trust in enterprises has risen in recent years based on the choice by chief executives to energetically engage in social issues. Consumer interest and apparent followings were created in public stances by Paul Polman of Unilever on the environment, Howard Schultz of Starbucks on youth employment, and Jack Ma of Alibaba on inclusion.

Despite these positive findings, the general population remains skeptical about the motivations of large enterprises. Yet in many ways business has the best chance of bridging the trust gap while still fulfilling its mandate to create value. According to the 2016 *Edelman Trust Barometer*, a decisive 80 percent of the general public expected that businesses can both increase profits and improve economic and social conditions in the communities in which they operate. The general population sees business as the institution best able to keep pace with rapid change, ranking it well above government and higher than nongovernmental organizations.

In the wake of the 2008 to 2009 "Great Recession," most business leaders tended to focus on their enterprise and short-term performance. Such a narrow focus is no longer practical. Modern, effective leadership means moving beyond the "grand illusion" to engage the mass population and to align business with societal goals. Trust in institutions is no longer principally granted on the basis of hierarchy or title. The reputation failures of large institutions, such as Arthur Andersen or the Catholic Church, or recognizable brands like Martha Stewart and BP, have changed the nature of trust. In today's world, trust must be earned and maintained.

The Role of Enterprise Corporate Communication and Corporate Authenticity

Many observers and public relations/communication counselors consider effective communication to play the key role in overcoming crises. Certainly, for decades the enterprise corporate communication function has played a meaningful role in building and supporting an enterprise's identity and reputation. A meaningful fraction of these communications, especially in defensive situations such as brand crises, have been characterized—negatively—as "spin" by critics, the media, and affected stakeholders. In today's world, communication importantly includes the enterprise's website, where it can tell its side of the issue and establish a conversation/response capability.

At least two significant challenges confront efforts to make authenticity an enterprise reality—one situational and one generic. The former arises when corporations find themselves in defensive situations (e.g., under attack for corporate or executive actions/inactions). The latter is the systemic tendency for communication to overstate an enterprise's (or product/service brand's) likely performance via exaggeration or overpromise; this in turn can generate a "promise-performance gap" (Greyser and Diamond 1974) perceived over time by consumers, business-to-business customers, and/or other stakeholder groups. In some situations, stakeholder constituencies will accept some degree of exaggeration as a normal accompaniment of advertising and communication. In crisis situations, critics and media tend to examine enterprise response more closely in terms of content and time lag of response.

In reputation-intensive situations, the relevant receiving stakeholder constituencies typically base effective communication on a foundation of trust between the enterprise and its followers. Trust has become a key dimension in studies of corporate reputation, as well as examination of stakeholders' and opinion leaders' attitudes toward business and other institutions in society.

In its 2007 report, *The Authentic Enterprise*, the Page Society observed,

In a marketplace where access and institutional authority can no longer be controlled, expertise and authenticity become more crucial than ever before. Every enterprise must be grounded in a clear sense of itself. Indeed, an enterprise or institution that is sure of its purpose, mission and values—and that takes those bedrock definitions seriously—is effectively compelled to behave in ways that are consistent with its core values. (p. 16)

Perceived authenticity and a positive reputation go hand in hand. However, there are at least four contexts of authenticity, in all of which communication play a role along with other key dimensions of building, sustaining, and defending reputation. What connects them is the importance of substance: "substance is the foundation of effective communication, supported by authenticity" (Greyser May 2008). The four contexts are:

- Talking "authentic," which is communication.
- Being authentic, which is based on an enterprise's core values and its track record—that is, its behavior. (Urde, Greyser, and Balmer 2007; Urde 2009)
- Staying authentic, which calls on an enterprise's stewardship of its core values.
- Defending authenticity in times of trouble, which draws on an enterprise's "reputational reservoir" and the trust it has generated over time. (Greyser 2009)

Again, substance—in the form of enterprise corporate behavior past and present—undergirds its ability to talk, be, and stay authentic, in normal as well as troubled times. Similarly, the substance of an enterprise's response is the most significant element of a crisis situation. *Acta, non verba*—deeds, not words—is Greyser's (2008) reminder that communication can be important in crises but content is more so. Further, enterprise credibility—based on corporate behavior and the performance of its products and services—is at the center of protecting the enterprise from the many unanticipated reputational problems it may confront, especially those not impacting on brand essence. The Page Model, as illustrated in *Building Belief* (2014), goes further in noting that authenticity is based on corporate character—the differentiating identity of the enterprise. If reputation is the shadow, corporate character is the tree. To strain the metaphor, authenticity is perhaps the root system, grounding the enterprise, providing stability and nourishment; trust is the fruit. Brand essence is the tree's core—its heart—that differentiates the brand, for example "efficacy" for a pain reliever, "faith" for a religion.

Without a platform of evidence-based substantive support, communication itself cannot leap the tall buildings of reputational trouble. With such support, communication can be effective. Together they build trust for the organization. Consider a university perceived as an institution with little meaningful research, despite a number of potentially significant projects and faculty publications. A communication-based program of managed visibility may help—including press releases on important publications, interviews with productive faculty, and substantive research conferences directed to relevant academic audiences. These signal (but do not and should not say) "we are important to knowledge in this field."

Trust and Sustainable Communication

In recent times, trust in enterprise values often encompasses sustainability issues.[1] It is helpful to provide contextual relevance and current practices to support CCO leadership in sustainability—which wraps around environmental or "green"—communication.

The term *sustainability communication* generally embraces enterprise efforts to connect with stakeholders on environmental, energy, product/service safety, and related matters that influence stakeholder trust and tie into enterprise risk management.

Stakeholder opinion of enterprise responsibilities is clear and enduring. Edelman's 2016 global trust survey confirmed, as it had in previous years, that environmental impact remains a strong factor in company-relevant social issues posing ongoing reputational risks.[2] Ranking of the environment among high-risk social issues has become a staple, at times surprising trend watchers. Tierney (May 17, 2014), writing in *The Atlantic*, revealed that American millennials were placing "government action protecting the environment from pollution" at least slightly above "action to protect the rights of women and minorities."[3]

Manufacturers, associations, service providers, and other enterprises commonly face, or embrace and depend upon, various aspects of sustainability, which began in environmental issues of the 1960s. At that

---

[1] The EPA (2014) has defined the organizing principle for sustainable development as connecting four domains: ecology, economics, politics, and culture. See graphic   https://epa.gov/sites/production/files/2014-10/documents/framework-for-sustainability-indicators-at-epa.pdf

[2] The Edelman 2016 survey cited "Gaps in Trust-Building Behaviors" with lapsing transparency in reporting progress on social responsibilities, such as quality control, safety, sustainability, and cause-oriented work. http://edelman.com/insights/intellectual-property/2016-edelman-trust-barometer/turbulent-times-call-for-new-strategies-in-building-trust/

[3] Survey cited in *Atlantic Magazine* (2014, May 17) article, "How to Win Millennials: Equality, Climate Change, and Gay Marriage," by John Tierney. While "pollution" can be case-specific, millennials apply the relevance of major green issues such as business-sector impact on climate change to virtually all enterprises. http://theatlantic.com/politics/archive/2014/05/everything-you-need-to-know-about-millennials-political-views/371053/

time waves of ecology[4] concerns put many enterprises in conflict with public opinion, and environmental advocates focused on "sustainability" as an extension of environmental and product safety. Sustainability, as a generalized topic addressing many enterprise/public issues, including environmental, has become a management fixture in many companies, with "sustainability officers" working alongside CCOs (see: http://sustainability.com/).

Green/sustainability and the rise of eco-concern can be traced to a book published in 1962. *Silent Spring*, by marine biologist Rachel Carson, imagined a future tragedy: a spring when birds, poisoned by pesticides, could not sing—and pointed to a villain: companies making crop-protecting pesticides. In a period of post-Vietnam agitation, protecting the environment became a cause, and chemical and allied product manufacturers became the earliest to communicate on environmental enterprise issues, strengths, and actions. The industry launched a *Responsible Care* program and chief executives were private sector leaders in the first United Nations sustainability conference.

Enterprise and political action shaped adoption of the 1969 Environmental Policy Act (1969), committing U.S. private and public sectors to sustainability and "fulfilling the social, economic and other requirements of present and future generations." An order from President Richard Nixon in1969 created America's front line of enforcement, the U.S. Environmental Protection Agency.[5]

---

[4] For many in both industry and media, the first indicator of pro-environment activism was in the late 1970s when the words "ecology now!" appeared on the United Nations plaza in New York, painted by anonymous, presumably early-green activists.

[5] President Nixon's 1970 reorganization plan set up the Environmental Protection Agency with William D. Ruckelshaus as first EPA administrator. Ruckelshaus subsequently served as FBI acting director, Deputy Attorney General; after EPA's 1983 debacle on the agency's action on Superfund cases, he returned to head EPA administrator; he subsequently served on corporate boards: Weyerhaeuser, Nordstrom, Monsanto, and Solutia.

With government empowerment and elevated public demand, enterprise engagement rose. In the spring of 1970, New York City's first "Earth Day" was celebrated. Volunteers staging the event were led by Marilyn Laurie, a mom and independent communicator, who would later become top communication officer at AT&T, and a major force in building the Arthur W. Page Society.[6]

Investors have spurred enterprise green economics. Enterprise action to avoid or fix environmental, food safety, and other areas of investment risk has become part of shareowner watch lists for more than three decades. Company communicators helped shape enterprise perspectives, pledges, and connections. Monsanto Company, manufacturer of chemical crop protectants, a primary target of eco-activists since the 1962 *Silent Spring* clarion, was a leader in enterprise leadership communication. At its 1970 annual meeting, CEO Charles H. Sommer told investors and financial news media: "Rhetoric about pollution abounds. If this helps describe the problems and force solutions it is helpful...yet there is a tremendous gap between rhetoric and commitment." He described the company's commitments in technology and the company's open response to "public insistence on action."[7] Investor attention to green/sustainability has produced pressure on enterprise leadership. Shareowner resolutions, such as the *Valdez Principles* (Ceres n.d.; Synacor 2015) generated by activist investors following the 1989 tanker oil spill in Valdez, Alaska, have compelled financial management and communication attention,

---

[6] Marilyn Laurie, later to join AT&T and become an officer and CCO, convinced Mayor John Lindsay to kick off the 1970 event for the pragmatic rationalization that many politicians as well as enterprise executives need to engage with environmental challenges. "(He) recognized," Laurie told an Arthur Page Society colleague in 2007, "that it was a better thing to be in front of than to be behind or against" (Harrison 2008, p. 165).

[7] Source for this is Dan J. Forrestal, in the 1960s the director, public relations, Monsanto, and a strong leader of chemical industry public relations people who came together following the Rachel Carson 1962 book (its thrust made first in an article in *New Yorker Magazine*).

and have influenced risk management reporting in annual Securities and Exchange Commission (SEC) 10-K reports.

Given these new realities, today's CCO must include the topic of sustainability as one of the imperatives in planning a communication program. This communication begins with listening to both stakeholders and critics. The "mutual gains" rule of conflict resolution: Remember the lessons, especially best outcomes achieved as the result of challengers.[8]

The basis for enterprise trust on environmental, health, safety, food safety, and all other products and services is simple: *show your evidence*. The communication with stakeholders boils down to a message delivered by an American company executive at the dawn of international pressure for industry environmental performance and sustainability. American and European CEOs participating in the 1992 UN sustainable development conference in Rio de Janeiro, Brazil, offered to begin opening their records on emissions measurement. External, qualified inspectors and the public would have access to emissions levels at the points of manufacturing. Executives said the purpose would be to show improvement in pollution controls. The talking point expressed by the CEOs is evergreen: "Don't trust us. *Track us*." That communication guide—openness, evidence, proof—is the basis for belief in enterprise shared-values, authenticity, and consequently earning trust. In this regard, the Environmental Protection Agency (Fiksel, Eason, and Frederickson October, 2012) has defined the organizing principle for sustainable development as connecting four domains: ecology, economics, politics, and culture (see Figure 3.1).

---

[8] Enterprise communicators can use guidance of the MIT-Harvard Public Disputes Program which has for 20 years been worked to test new and better ways of resolving public disputes. "We are particularly interested in disputes at the local, state, and national levels concerning the allocation of scarce resources (like land or water), the setting of policy priorities (Shall we emphasize economic development vs. environmental protection?), and the formulation of health and safety standards (What is an acceptable level of risk?)." See http://web.mit.edu/ publicdisputes/pdr/

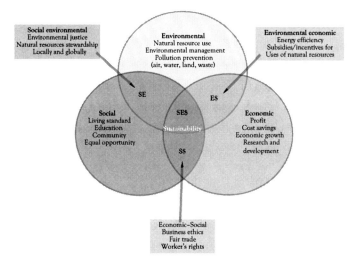

Figure 3.1 Sustainability. Used with permission of the Environmental Protection Agency

Source: https://epa.gov/sites/production/files/2014-10/documents/framework-for-sustainability-indicators-at-epa.pdf

Case: When Words Become Actions—The General Motors Ignition Switch Controversy

Trust is not an endpoint; it is a continuum. Trust between an organization and its stakeholders ebbs and flows over time, based on the actions of the organization and the reaction of those affected by it. General Motors (GM) experienced this in a powerful way in 2014 when an ignition switch defect surfaced that led to the recall of 2.6 million U.S.-built small cars, multiple state and federal investigations, thousands of legal claims for personal injury, death and economic loss, and fines and settlements totaling more than $2.1 billion.

The origin of this crisis was a relatively inexpensive part: the ignition switch. In the fall of 2002, an engineer approved a design that did not meet GM's internal specification for torque resistance. In other words, it was too easy to turn. The problem was this: if the key was jarred with enough force it could turn on its own and stall the car.

It was not long after the first cars went on sale as 2003 models that customer complaints started to surface. But the company's engineers and lawyers did not consider moving stalls to be a safety defect at the time, so a recall was not conducted. What they failed to understand was that a stall also cut power to the airbags, meaning they might not deploy in an accident.

Ultimately, it took more than 11 years for GM to fully establish the connection between inadvertent key rotation and airbag nondeployment, and recall the vehicles despite a stream of customer complaints. Among the many reasons: reports of airbag nondeployments dropped dramatically after 2006 and no one could explain why—not until early 2012.

In April of that year, lawyers representing the family of a Georgia woman who died in a crash uncovered something shocking: the same engineer who approved the substandard part in 2002 ordered changes in 2006 that increased torque in the switch, which effectively reduced the risk of inadvertent key rotation.

For reasons he never explained, he did not change the part number and he also told GM investigators on several occasions over the years that the design never changed—critical errors that delayed the recalls for almost two years.

The case in Georgia settled before trial in September 2013 and, about six months later, GM started recalling cars to replace their ignition switches. Almost immediately, internal GM documents produced in the Georgia case started circulating among regulators, journalists, and elected officials, triggering a tsunami of media coverage around the world. Everyone demanded to know why it took GM so long to recall the cars.

At the center of the response to the crisis was Mary Barra, the CEO of GM who had been with the company for 35 years. GM's board had elected Barra as the company's first female chief executive in late 2013 and she assumed the role in January 2014. Only a month, later GM issued the first of many recalls connected to the ignition switch problem and the crisis defined Barra's first year as CEO.

In April 2014, Barra testified before Congress about the defect. In her testimony, Barra drew criticism from congressional members, victims' families, and others for her failure to provide satisfying answers as to why the company had not acted sooner to fix the problem and what it intended to do to make up for these mistakes.

During the hearings, Senator Barbara Boxer (Democrat, California) asked Barra why she never heard anything about the faulty ignition switches during her long tenure as an executive at GM. Showing frustration with Barra's response, Boxer exclaimed to her "You don't know anything about anything. If this is the new GM leadership, it's pretty lacking" (CBS News April 2, 2014).

However, in her remarks, Barra made two significant announcements. First she said that GM would hire Kenneth Feinberg to help the company address the issue of compensation for the victims' families. Feinberg had been widely praised for his role in many highly visible mass-injury cases, including the BP Gulf of Mexico oil spill and the Boston Marathon bombing.

She also announced that GM had hired former United States Attorney Anton Valukas to help the company develop a comprehensive understanding of why it took so long to initiate the recall. The hiring of both Feinberg and Valukas would prove to be key developments in GM's restoration of stakeholder trust.

The role of GM's corporate communication department was pivotal in developing the strategy for rebuilding credibility. In May 2014, long-time industry veteran Tony Cervone was brought in as senior vice president of global communication to lead the effort in coping with the crisis.

Cervone and his team molded their communication approach based on the enterprise strategy that Mary Barra and her team had developed. The strategy had three essential components as keys to recovery:

- Fix the vehicles.
- Do the right thing for customers.
- Hold GM accountable.

Through the recall program, GM began replacing the faulty ignition switches on millions of vehicles worldwide. The program was expanded several times to ensure that *all* vehicles with a potential risk were addressed. With the assistance of Feinberg, the company developed a program that offered millions of dollars in compensation to the victims. "We knew that we needed to hold ourselves fully accountable," says Cervone. "That meant accepting responsibility for what had happened and implementing actions to make sure that we fully addressed the reasons behind the failure."

In structuring the crisis response, the team developed a customer-oriented focus that centered on four areas:

- Communication
- Public policy
- Legal
- Sales and marketing

In all of these areas, Cervone emphasized that the team should feel both informed and empowered, by making sure all facts were on the table, roles and responsibilities were clearly defined, and the approval process was fast and responsive. "We knew that it was essential that we use a strategic, proactive process that would reduce surprises, move fast, anticipate reactions from key stakeholders and avoid self-inflicted wounds."

A key moment of truth in the crisis was the release of the *Valukas Report* (May 29, 2014). The report was highly critical of GM's actions in the ignition switch recall process. As reported in *The New York Times* (Vlasic June 5, 2014, pp. 3–4):

> The report illustrates in unsparing detail how employees across departments neglected for years to repair a defect and issue a recall, despite a mountain of evidence that lives were at risk. "Although everyone had responsibility to fix the problem, nobody took responsibility."
>
> —Mr. Valukas wrote

What is significant is the manner in which GM responded to the scathing report and in particular the sense of personal responsibility exhibited by Barra, who was highly visible during the release of the report, speaking candidly about the company's failures and mistakes to a global town hall gathering of employees—a meeting that media were invited to monitor.

She could not have been clearer in her assessment of the *Valukas* findings (Barras June 5, 2014, pp. 8–10):

> I can tell you the report is extremely thorough, brutally tough and deeply troubling. For those of us who have dedicated our lives to this company, it is enormously painful to have our shortcomings laid out so vividly. I was deeply saddened and disturbed as I read the report.

> But this isn't about our feelings or our egos. This is about our responsibility to act with integrity, honor and a commitment to excellence.

> With all of our colleagues around the world watching today, I want it known that this recall issue isn't merely an engineering or manufacturing or legal problem, it represents a fundamental failure to meet the basic needs of these customers.

Barra went to great lengths in her remarks to detail exactly what the company was doing to respond to the findings and to take meaningful actions to reduce the risk of such crises occurring again.

> As I prepared for today, I thought long and hard about the very tough message I would be delivering. I knew full well how difficult this experience would be for all of us. But I also knew the only course was to be direct and totally honest. This is a test of our character and our values. In the end, I'm not afraid of the truth, and I know you aren't either. I want it known that we will face up to our mistakes and take them head on. The fact is I believe in this company and I believe in you. I want GM to be the world's best automotive company—for customers. Whatever it takes to do that is what we are going to do. (pp. 53–55)

It was an impressive demonstration of CEO accountability. While the words were powerful, the actions spoke even louder. Fifteen GM employees were dismissed, some for incompetence, some for misconduct, and some for simply being too slow or insensitive in their response to the situation, and five were disciplined. The company paid close to $600 million in settlements with 400 accident victims who may have been injured or killed in a switch-related accident, and paid $900 million in settlement with the U.S. government. GM also implemented a comprehensive new approach to safety, consolidating safety responsibilities under a corporate vice president and hiring 35 new safety investigators.

The communication function learned many valuable lessons from the crisis. They are now better prepared to assess the company's risks and vulnerabilities. They have also gained a new appreciation for the company's strengths, including the significant changes implemented as a result of the *Valukas Report* findings and GM's response to them.

In the ensuing months since the crisis first surfaced, GM has seen many positive developments as a result of the strong actions taken. But the company executives are keenly aware that the crisis is far from over. While the majority of the settlement issues have been completed, individual lawsuits will take years to resolve.

It has been a painful and costly reminder that the actions of a handful of employees can have a profound impact on an enterprise's reputation. Any enterprise can be susceptible to mistakes by individuals, but it is ultimately judged by how it responds to these mistakes, makes meaningful changes to repair the damage, and ensures that it is doing everything in its power to reduce the risk of such mistakes happening in the future.

Preserving Trust: A Journey Not a Destination

The key to restoring trust, and preserving reputational capital, lies in following some fairly basic principles. Like all such maxims, these are easy to say, harder to do. First and foremost, follow the first two Page Principles: *Tell the truth* and *Prove it with action*. That seems obvious, but the challenge rests with defining what is "truthful." For example, most enterprises are under enormous pressure from shareholders to meet quarterly profit goals. This pressure is often passed down the line, tempting lower level managers to cross the line in what they report regarding sales, orders, or costs (see Wells Fargo). They may feel they are acting in the company's best interests but in the end this deception is likely to be revealed, causing further damage to the organization's reputation and compromising stakeholders' trust.

Truth also is essential when communicating job expectations to employees and providing timely feedback about performance. Employees are often given very little information about job expectations, yet managers are surprised when those they supervise do not deliver the expected results. Employees simply want to know exactly what is expected of them; they want to hear praise when they have delivered and they want plenty of warning—and time to make improvements—if they are not measuring up. Most employees also want to know how their unit is performing and where the company is headed. If these communication expectations are met, employees will be far more likely to offer suggestions on how things can be done more productively.

External stakeholders, such as customers, are not much different. They want a square deal, straight talk, and a commitment to back up promises made. Chipotle restaurants endured a long battle with foodborne illnesses recently and management made the difficult decision to shut down the entire operation for a day to focus on communicating about restaurant cleanliness and illness prevention. It was a costly decision and the chain is not yet out of the woods, but their commitment demonstrates what it takes to restore confidence.

In today's rapidly changing world, the CCO must also make it easy for stakeholders to connect with her enterprise. It is inescapable that the number of people who access the Internet through devices other than personal computers, including tablets, smartphones, and connected TVs, will continue to increase exponentially.

Younger professionals—generally grouped as millennials—have become a strong factor in enterprise views and communication. Millennial opinion informs and influences stakeholder options about buying from, investing in, and working for enterprises that do not meet their expectations about what is morally and socially acceptable (see Chapters 4 and 9). Technological connectivity shapes their attitudes and actions. Capable engagement in these exchanges, with millennials directly involved, is a key to successful enterprise communication.

Acting ethically sometimes means walking away from business, and it rarely is the cheapest way to go to market. But in the long run the price the enterprise pays for behaving unethically overwhelms the costs of doing the right thing. Authentic behavior also enhances employee pride, improves retention of customers and employees, and builds trust among all stakeholders. In the end, it is better for business. Just ask Volkswagen, Toshiba, Valeant, Wells Fargo, or any enterprise that has paid a high price for ethical lapses.

Although the CEO is the ultimate guardian of an enterprise's trust and reputation, the CCO can (and should) serve as their internal custodian, and as monitor and protector of its "trust quotient." Trust must be earned and re-earned with every customer transaction and contact and reaffirmed with every stakeholder interaction (even if the stakeholder is not a friend). To do this calls for constant concern and concentration. It is hard work. Alas, there is no app for "trust."

Summary

Successful relationships depend on trust—trust between spouses, trust between parent and child, trust between enterprises and their stakeholders. This chapter focused on the factors that build trust in organizations, as well as the forces that can diminish or destroy it, and the role of enterprise communication in managing these forces.

The chapter included a discussion of the most relevant findings from the annual *Edelman Trust Barometer*, a bellwether of measuring trust and relationships between a company and its stakeholders. This was explored in detail through a case where General Motors dealt with a serious recall crisis translated these concepts into the reality of managing a global enterprise in a trustworthy manner.

CHAPTER 4

Managing the Corporate Character of the Enterprise: Identity, Purpose, Culture, and Values

Shannon A. Bowen, Ginger Hardage, and Wendi Strong

Previous chapters noted that enterprises and brands are perceived by their stakeholder as if they have personal qualities.[1] These qualities—values and culture—make up what would be called their *character*. This chapter focuses directly on what corporate character is and the factors that impact how enterprises create and convey values, leading to decisions that affect the organization and stakeholders. An important part of the enterprise model focuses on how corporate character is created and the role of the chief communication officer (CCO) in establishing, maintaining, and altering enterprise character.

What is corporate character? Character is viewed as being tied to the values, beliefs, and credos the enterprise presents to its stakeholders, as noted in a Page Society white paper (Arthur W. Page Society, 2013b):

---

[1] Organizations who agreed to have their communications efforts discussed in this chapter were Southwest Airlines and USAA. We wish to thank and acknowledge these organizations for their pioneering spirit and allowing us to discuss the proprietary examples contained in this chapter. The researchers wish to thank the Arthur W. Page Society and the numerous Page committees who have constructed white papers that were valuable in our research.

[L]eading companies take a deliberate approach to corporate character by systematically defining, activating and aligning their *values* [emphasis added] with their operations. Moreover, these processes involve an enterprise-wide set of activities that require support and coordination across the C-Suite, preferably with input from employees and a central role for the CCO. (p. 5)

Further, it is an essential function of the CCO to help drive an organization toward living those values or to advocate change when alignment with values is needed:

Although the alignment process is more business and operational in nature, in a number of companies the CCO fulfills a substantial leadership role in the effort, alongside other C-Suite executives, to help the organization not only to "look like" and "sound like" its values, but also to "think like" and "perform like" its stated character. (Arthur W. Page Society 2013c, p. 8)

Ethical responsibility and rectitude, a growing skepticism and lack of trust among stakeholders, and increasing demands for accountability highlight the reasons that values and corporate character are at the center of creating identity. Demands for transparency probably derived from accounting scandals, such as Enron, and actually meant that stakeholders wanted clarity in financial procedures. But along with clarity, the CCO helps to create a corporate character based on ethical values, a clear mission and vision, and a strong organizational culture (Bowen 2010; Bowen and Heath 2005; Standish 2012). And, that culture must hold fit or alignment with organizational values and actions.

What Is Corporate Identity?

Values and character are inextricably linked to enterprise *identity*. Examining what that identity is and how it arises allows us to understand how corporate character can be used to create a positive identity and reputation, as well as a competitive advantage in the marketplace. According to

Balmer and Greyser (2003), Mukherjee and He (2008) described three attributes of identity:

> First, company identity should capture the essence of the company—the criterion of claim central character. Second, company identity should distinguish the company from others—the criterion of claim distinctiveness. Third, company identity should exhibit some degree of sameness or continuity over time—the criterion of claimed temporal endurance. (p. 111)

Although Fombrun (1996) described identity as a concept associated with reputation, and Mukherjee and He (2008) defined it as one linked to marketing, scholars have long agreed that enterprise identity influences stakeholder reactions to both cognitive assessments and behavioral outcomes of strategic issues. Going a step further, Dutton and Penner (1993) found that enterprise identity held implications for strategic performance through the process of agenda building. J. E. Grunig (1992a, 2011) argued that identity can be created inside an organization although reputation is external to it and cannot be managed. Identity and reputation are, perhaps, best conceptualized as two sides of the same coin.

Identity is a crucial concept to building a competitive advantage or achieving organizational effectiveness. Scholars agree that the concept is amorphous and fluid (Ashforth and Mael 1989), although terms such as identity, image, core values, and reputation are all used and contested in the literature. The concept—despite being difficult to define—is clearly salient. Identity has an impact on both how stakeholders view an enterprise and on its competitive performance in the marketplace. A case is helpful to illustrate how research was used to define and refine identity at United Services Automobile Association (USAA).

Case: USAA Defining Corporate Character

Corporate character is the perfect descriptor of what USAA sought to define as it approached its 90th year in business. From humble beginnings in 1922, it grew into a Fortune-200, fully-diversified financial services company focused on the U.S. military community. USAA's mission was clear: to facilitate the financial security of military families. But, as the company capitalized on its strong financial position to aggressively grow awareness and market share during the Great Recession and the years following, it became clear that serving a much larger and more diverse market made it imperative for USAA to be able to convey the meaningful difference between it and its competitors.

USAA embarked on a journey of research, discovery, and introspection that yielded important insights. Key questions included: How was USAA currently perceived among its 11 million stakeholders, its members, and prospective customers? How did it wish to be perceived? Perhaps most importantly: *What was it about USAA that caused its members to be so passionate about it?*

Originally derived from military values, USAA's core values of service, honesty, loyalty, and integrity remained relevant with those of members. But awareness of USAA was *not* high among potential members; a flaw that could only be remedied once the company honed its identity.

The most profound findings came out of psychographic research to understand USAA members' devotion to the company. Again and again, USAA members used the word *love* to describe how they felt about USAA and how they believed USAA felt about them. Further research exposed three emotions that combined to create an extraordinarily strong customer–company relationship:

1. Members felt a powerful sense of *belonging* to an exclusive community. (Eligibility is established through a family connection to a military member.)
2. USAA's financial strength and sound financial advice were seen as key benefits that helped members feel *protected*.
3. Most critically, the empathy exhibited by employees led members to believe that the company put their needs ahead of its own. In short, members felt *cared for*.

Numerous research studies led to the creation of a newly invigorated and well-defined corporate character cementing USAA's position as a company devoted to those who have served our country. The outcome was a clearly articulated, meaningful, and unique character. The CEO at the time simply called it "Our rallying cry."

We Go Above For Those Who Have Gone Beyond
through
Shared Military Values
Financial Strength and Wisdom
Passionate Member Advocacy

Once these foundational pillars were established, USAA embarked on a multiyear journey to ensure every aspect of its business aligned with and enhanced its corporate character.

- Empathy became a key character quality, which call center managers sought and valued when hiring.
- Products were assessed to ensure alignment with corporate character. For instance, when viewed through the lens of character, foreign transaction fees on credit cards did not demonstrate advocacy for military members stationed around the world; the fees were eliminated.
- A new corporate responsibility strategy was created to reinforce USAA's commitment to the military and bring member advocacy to life. For example, a partnership was formed with the Elizabeth Dole Foundation to support military caregivers, a group underserved by other programs. And USAA became a leader in hiring veterans and working to end veteran' homelessness.
- A major initiative for the CCO, in partnership with the marketing and human resources departments, was to be sure that USAA's behavior, sound, identity, culture, and communication climate powerfully projected its character.

Enterprise Mission, Vision, and Purpose

Concepts often linked with enterprise identity are mission or purpose, vision, and values.[2] Values will be discussed in detail further in this chapter, yet no discussion of enterprise identity and character would be complete without examining the concept of *mission*. An enterprise's mission serves to clarify its purpose: why it exists and what its goals are. A mission is often based on a competitive advantage and communicated through a mission statement. Mission statements "are used as tools to convey goals, organizational structure, strategy, legitimacy, values, participation and ownership among employees, leadership, responsibility to the community, ethical priorities, and commitment to publics and stakeholders" (Bowen 2005, p. 536). The *vision* of the enterprise is longer term, broader, and more aspirational in nature. "[A] vision spells out a target for change and the desired long-term goal state" (Bowen 2005, p. 535). A shared vision of where the organization would like to be often motivates internal stakeholders to innovate and drive toward longer term goals.

For instance, USAA's mission and vision are combined in its mission statement:

> The mission of USAA is to facilitate the financial security of its members, associates and their families by providing a full range of financial products and services *(mission)*; in so doing, USAA seeks to be the provider of choice for the military community *(vision)*.

Similarly, the Southwest Airlines mission statement incorporates a long-range, strategic goal. While Southwest Airlines is the largest *domestic* airline based on number of passengers carried (118 million in 2015), the company's vision statement reflects a longer-term view (Southwest Airlines n.d.):

---

[2] Brand identity is a common term as well, but is specific to a brand; organizational identity is much broader as it refers to an organization that may produce numerous brands, each with their own brand identity. The two terms are, therefore, not synonymous.

Vision—Become the world's most loved, most flown, and most profitable airline.

Mission—The mission of Southwest Airlines is dedication to the highest quality of Customer Service delivered with a sense of warmth, friendliness, individual pride, and Company Spirit.

Both mission and vision are related to corporate character because they are based on its core values and give it driving purpose. A mission statement can be used in operational decision making to clarify organizational priorities and goals; a vision statement can be used to help determine priorities for change and innovation. Basing mission and vision on the enterprise core values fosters a strong organizational identity, eventually resulting in a consistent corporate character, allowing it to be known externally in the marketplace and to organize team- and goal-oriented behavior internally.

Case: Southwest Airlines: Bringing Purpose to Life in an Organization

In January 2013, Southwest Airlines unveiled the following corporate purpose: We exist to connect people to what's important in their lives through friendly, reliable, and low-cost air travel (http://investors.southwest.com/ourcompany/purpose_vision_alues_and_mission).

Storytelling became the most effective way to educate Southwest Airlines employees on the company's purpose and to continue to reinforce that purpose in their day-to-day interactions with customers. On Southwest's YouTube channel, through internal news channels, and on its blog, Nuts about Southwest, the airline posts articles and videos to bring its purpose statement to life. Through seemingly everyday situations, the company's goal is to display how employees go above and beyond to connect people to what's important in their lives.

In one YouTube video, Jessica, a Southwest Airlines customer, talks about the day she and her family saw her husband off for a six-month deployment to Kuwait. Kelli, a Southwest Airlines customer service agent, saw the family and asked if they wanted special clearance to go to the gate. "It bought us thirty more minutes to spend time together," customer Jessica said. Yet another employee asked if the family would like to go on the plane. The father headed for Kuwait was able to give his family one last hug while the entire plane of passengers cheered for them. At the end of the video, Jessica says into the camera, "Because of you, me and my family have a memory for a lifetime." This is just one example of how storytelling reinforces behavior and helps employees visualize what the company's purpose can look and feel like.

Enterprise Core Values: Ethics, Beliefs, and Action

Core values are the ethical beliefs, norms, and standards that are held by an enterprise and the people in it. They are the ethical principles deemed to be worthy of action in an enterprise. Essentially, ethics determine core values and core values are our manifestation of ethics through action and management decision making.

High-performing organizations normally spend a great deal of resources defining and refining core values (Bowen 2002; Sims 1994; Goodpaster 2007) because they help unify and advance strategic management (Bowen 2004) and strategic communication (Botan 1997; Heath 2006). Core values of an organization can be summarized and listed in a statement, checklist, or other decision-making tool that ensures ethics are included in strategic management. How ethical values are defined, discussed, and demonstrated ultimately influences the nature of ethical decision making within an enterprise and yield perceptions of its character. Further, refining the way we understand and discuss ethics is particularly important in delineating core values because they are rather static and slow to change in most organizations (Sims 1994).

Individual Versus Organizational Ethics

Ethical reasoning is an incredibly complex construct that one should not oversimplify. To understand how corporate character is created, based upon its foundational component of core values combined with other variables such as identity, mission, vision, and culture, it is necessary to examine where ethics and core values originate. Are they organizational or individual?

We can classify ethics as occurring at four levels: the individual, group, enterprise level, and cultural or societal levels (Sims 1994).

According to Sims (1994), these four levels of ethics allow us to study the predominant or primary context in which ethical decisions are made. However, there is overlap because enterprises are made up of individuals who apply the enterprise's ethical framework, a group decision-making framework, and their own individual moral values to ethical problems, within a societal context.[3] Perhaps the question most germane to this chapter is can individual ethics be applied, creating a corporate *character* via the level of enterprise ethics? Because these ethical theories are intended to be generally and broadly applicable across every conceivable situation, the answer is: *yes*.

The debate between individual ethics and corporate ethics has been described as factious, and responsible for much criticism of business. As Seeger (1997) explains: "Viewing the individual as the only moral agent tends to release the organization from an ethical obligation" (p. 8). He further notes that courts, laws, and CEOs often acknowledge social responsibilities and obligations. DeGeorge (2010) argues that regulatory actions will impose accountability where it does not exist, therefore the argument is largely a moot debate. However, regulatory action and legal compliance are not substitutes for ethical accountability (Bowen 2010; Bowen and Heath 2005; Sims 1994).

The enterprise and its stakeholders are perhaps best viewed as ethical points on a continuous loop rather than competing opposites. As DeGeorge (2007) explains: "Moral people are needed to create and sustain moral structures. The two reinforce each other" (p. 110). Further, it has been argued that the firm must go beyond pure profit motives to see enterprises as collectives who are responsible for ethical behavior (DeGeorge 2010; French and Weis 2000; Seeger 1997).

Organizations can be understood as having cultures that arise as greater constructs, with the whole greater than the sum of its parts, from

---

[3] For an extended discussion of these dynamics and problematics, see Sims (1994).

the individual moral actors within them, combined with core values. Scholars (Goodpaster 2007; Seeger 1997; Sims 1994) argued that an organization can have a conscience and even a moral intention that can be studied and has been modeled (Goodpaster 2007, pp. 76, 83).

Enterprise Corporate Conscience

Moral conscience is both an individual concept and one that can be applied collectively, as moral awareness and insight requiring the coordination of self-interest alongside respect for others (Goodpaster 2007, p. 53). In the sense that ethics are primarily organizational and intentional, a corporate conscience exists independently of the actors who comprise it. However, organizations are comprised of individuals with their own values that sometimes compete with or conflict with those of peer groups and management—sometimes for the better, as an activist for ethical behavior, and sometimes for the worse. The potential for negative outcomes increases through stifling of individual moral autonomy or "groupthink," retribution, pressure, denial of responsibility, and so on. Many infamous cases of ethical breaches, such as the Volkswagen deception in emissions testing, may result (Bowen, Stacks, and Wright 2017). Individuals with strong moral values and an enterprise culture that considers ethics (Sims 1994; Bowen 2004) each help create a corporate conscience, with the CCO acting as an ethical conscience (Ryan and Martinson 1988).

Further, Trevino (1986) found that organizational culture, rewards and punishments, situational factors, and locus of control all exert more influence on ethics than did individual ethical standards; enterprise ethics take precedence over personal ethics as a form of insurance against self-interested or unethical behaviors. Sims (1994) explained that compromising one's personal beliefs in the interests of enterprise ethical standards was *positively related to managerial success* (p. 21). It is not enough that an enterprise be made up of ethical individuals and hold a strong organizational culture; it also must be an organizational culture that values ethics and seeks to act with good moral intention (Goodpaster 2007). It is not enough to hope that a corporate conscience exists; it must be institutionalized or created as a part of its very structure and culture of the enterprise, discussed in the next section of this chapter.

The CCO should act as the corporate conscience in the enterprise, advising CEOs and management on the ethics of its actions. CCOs are especially suited to perform this role because they maintain relationships with many stakeholders, both internal and external, across functional areas, and they understand the varied priorities and values of those groups. Worldwide, professional communicators reported that they *are* performing the role of ethical conscience in their organizations (Bowen et al. 2006) and that they believe communication is the appropriate function from which to advise on ethics (Bowen 2008). CCOs explain their relation to ethics as one that is natural based on enterprise reputation (Bowen 2012; Grunig 2006), building trust among strategic publics (Bowen, Hung-Baesecke, and Chen 2016), and the necessary yet skeptical relationships they have with journalists (Bowen 2016).

Enterprise Culture (Corporate Culture)

Enterprise culture can be conceptualized as how we act or do things in an enterprise, including the internal communication climate and core values that comprise its character. The character of an organization is displayed through its culture and behaviors that emanate from it.[4] Factors that create an organization's culture include: the amount of formalization or bureaucracy; stratification; the value placed on autonomy and teamwork; power distance; nature of collaboration or division of labor; codification of policies; attention to ethics; the value of employees; stewardship and social responsibility; and style of leadership.

When conceptualized as a continuum, most enterprises can be categorized, to a predominant degree, as more participative or more authoritarian (Smircich and Calas 1987; Weick 1987). Authoritarian cultures

---

[4] Part of the rationale for this list is simply for the sake of brevity. The socioeconomic conditions of a society can influence how one *sees* the world and *interacts* (behaves) within an enterprise culture. For example, those in totalitarian societies have a collective worldview and are reluctant to take individual responsibility; whereas the worldview of Westerners places heightened emphasis on personal accountability. Worldviews are components of how the individual navigates an organizational role and operates within a larger organizational culture.

are those with a high preference toward structured authority, stratified hierarchy, formalized bureaucracy, a centralized organizational structure, individualized responsibilities, and a reliance on standard operating procedures and policies (Jablin 1987). Conversely, participative cultures are the opposite: teamwork and innovation are encouraged, a decentralized or matrix organizational structure is normally present, employees are encouraged to share responsibility, innovate, and share input, and less bureaucracy and lower levels of stratification and codified authority or formal hierarchy are seen (Siebold and Shea 2001).

The factors of culture combined to generate smaller and more specific zones of meaning inside an enterprise. A smaller and more specific *communication climate* exists in units or groups throughout the work environment (McPhee and Poole 1983). Communication climates, which range from supportive to defensive and sometimes open to closed (Stacks, Hickson, and Hill 1991), can vary from enterprise culture and are unique to smaller units of the overall firm. Many different communication climates can simultaneously exist throughout an enterprise because they differ across areas, units, or groups (Poole and McPhee 1983). Communication climates are partial determinants of the kind of culture inside an enterprise, and the importance of an ethical climate, which encourages open discussion and transparency, cannot be overstated (Shin 2012). Communication climate should be open to encourage the free discussion of values and ideas, problem solving, and information sharing as part of a strong character.

Often participative cultures hold advantages for employees when compared to cultures that are authoritarian (Siebold and Shea 2001; Smircich and Calas 1987; Sriramesh, Grunig, and Buffington 1992). In participative cultures, employees experience greater support, motivation, effectiveness, and retention levels than in authoritarian cultures (Grunig 1992b; Grunig, Grunig, and Dozier 2002). Ethically speaking, an advantage is held by participative cultures because they emphasize the value of people, use open communication climates, encourage innovation, welcome input, and offer more supportive relational factors than by authoritarian culture (Grunig 1992b). Because it is based on efficiency, formalization, and routinization, an authoritarian culture can create low levels of motivation and job satisfaction, resulting in employee turnover.

Authoritarian cultures can hold more closed or even foreboding communication climates that limit the identification and discussion of ethical issues. To encourage strong character, enterprises should work toward an inclusive, participative culture and open communication climate, as these factors also increase employee motivation, satisfaction, and retention (Grunig et al. 2002). Importantly, a participative culture often values the role of communication and includes a corporate conscience counselor role for the CCO (Bowen 2008). As a conscience counselor, the CCO can use ethical frameworks to advise the CEO and management on dilemmas of values and character (Bowen, Rawlins, and Martin 2010).

Leadership is another factor that plays a role in determining culture, especially from the CEO (Harrison and Mühlberg 2014). The CCO plays an important role in communicating initiatives, yet the CEO drives the mission and day-to-day operations. Therefore, the CEO is often the most important actor in creating an ethical organizational culture. As Goodpaster (2007) argues, "The leader is the principal architect of corporate conscience and the one who must ... give substance to the moral agenda of the organized group. That agenda includes orienting, institutionalizing, and sustaining conscience in the corporate culture" (p. 7). The CEO sets the tone for corporate character, but an ethical conscience must be *involved* in the process before it can be sustained in the enterprise's culture. That is the role for the CCO of the future— and many CCOs are doing that now (Bowen 2009).

Establishing the Enterprise Culture

In 2006, Trevino, Weaver, and Reynolds documented numerous positive outcomes of ethical enterprise behavior and culture—in perceptions (internal and external, e.g., fairness, rectitude), in ethical behavior (e.g., monitoring, reporting), and in actual organizational performance (e.g., measures of success, profit, retention). In essence, ethics matters and makes a difference to how profitable an enterprise is—and can be. To become an integral part of an organization's character, ethics and core values must be integrated into the corporate culture. According to Goodpaster (2007), the steps for integrating ethics into a culture are: orienting, institutionalizing, and sustaining shared ethical values.

Orienting

Orienting an enterprise culture toward strong ethical character involves determining and refining its core values. Those core values may be a source of debate or disagreement, but internal research should be conducted to determine what employees at all levels believe are enterprise core values. Are our core values in *alignment* with the mission and vision of the enterprise? Volk and Zerfass (2017) defined *alignment* as the "degree of linkage between the communication strategy and the overall organizational strategy" (p. 15) as well as between activities and goals.

Core values can be refined and re-examined with alignment in mind, always with the input of internal stakeholders at all levels (Men and Bowen 2017). Doing so not only accomplishes inclusion of their ideas, but it creates a commitment to the enterprise and a genuine feeling of value among employees. The following case is a good example of orienting an organizational culture.

Case: USAA—Aligning Values, Culture, and Character

USAA's core values of *service, loyalty, honesty, and integrity* are more than words on a page, they are used in daily decision making. Not only are these values literally carved in stone in USAA's home office, they are ingrained in its employees from the first moment of their three-day orientation.

Once USAA's corporate character was articulated, six tenets were developed to drive internal alignment between culture, values, and the newly refined character. *The USAA Standard* was introduced as a set of principles to which every employee should aspire:

- Keep our membership and mission first.
- Live our core values: service, loyalty, honesty, and integrity.
- Be authentic and build trust.
- Create conditions for people to succeed.
- Purposefully include diverse perspectives for superior results.
- Innovate and build for the future.

> The *Standard* encompasses USAA's mission, values, and aspirations, and is helping maintain the company's unique culture and shape it for the future. Employees who live the *Standard* are publicly recognized. The tenets are discussed regularly in meetings, and decisions are made based on them. And performance evaluations have been modified to focus equally on *how* people achieve results and *what* they accomplish.

Institutionalization

The second step of instilling ethics into the culture of an enterprise is *institutionalization* (Goodpaster 2007). Institutionalization involves adopting and formalizing the set of core values as discovered or refining it after a number of years. It also involves using and integrating those values throughout the organization, a process that some call "activating corporate character" (Sims 1994). The CCO plays a vital role in the institutionalization of ethics through using the internal relations function. Communicating about the enterprise's values is only one step of the process. Institutionalization also involves training internal stakeholders (employees and management) on core values, modeling values-driven behavior, and using case studies to discuss potential scenarios. It includes building incentive and reward systems for following core values, using core values as a standard part of the annual review process, offering an anonymous question and answer space for concerns, and designing policies and penalties for infractions. Leading enterprises designate specific awards for praiseworthy behavior in this area. The best enterprises create tools that integrate values into routine decision making (at operations and managerial levels), but they are especially helpful for use by the CCO in managing ethical issues. When core values are known and used in routine discussion, decision making, evaluations, reporting, internal communication, and modeled through behavior of both employees and leadership, values have been institutionalized.

Southwest Airlines offers an exemplary look at how to institutionalize a value-driven organizational culture.

Case: Southwest Airlines—Institutionalization of Values

The values of Southwest Airlines are referred to as "Living the Southwest Way" and are used as a guidepost beginning with hiring through evaluation of job performance. These values are unique to the character of Southwest Airlines and include specific descriptions so expected behavior is clear to everyone within the organization.

Warrior Spirit

> Never give up
> Strive to be the best
> Protect our Profitsharing

Servant's Heart

> Treat others with respect
> Follow the Golden Rule
> Embrace our Southwest Family

Fun-LUVing Attitude

> Be a passionate Team Player
> Celebrate successes
> Don't take yourself too seriously

Through various on-boarding tools (e.g., interactive, online education), employees learn early in their careers about the importance of carrying out Southwest Airlines' values. The values are further reinforced when employees attend orientation at the Training and Operational Support (TOPS) building, a 492,000 square-foot building dedicated to initial and continuing education of its people.

The values appear prominently at all Southwest Airlines locations, but are especially visible at the Dallas-based headquarters where 16 "Culture Centers" bring the company's character to life and showcase

20,000 pieces of historic memorabilia. For example, the Fun-LUVing Attitude Culture Center graphically displays life-size photographic murals and colorful quotes from Founder and Chairman Emeritus Herb Kelleher. Known for his sense of humor, this Culture Center includes a "laugh button" so visitors can personally hear Kelleher's hearty laugh amplified. The area includes space for employees to meet, enjoy a meal, and even play foosball while learning about what it means to display a Fun-LUVing Attitude.

The department responsible for creating these Culture Centers is the Culture Services Department, but their scope includes many other responsibilities. The culture is of such importance and prominence at Southwest Airlines that this novel department is dedicated to nurturing, celebrating, recognizing, and preserving its uniqueness and corporate character.

Sustaining

The third and final step of creating a culture that expresses character is *sustaining shared ethical values* throughout the enterprise (Goodpaster 2007). It is important to note that the process of sustaining shared ethical values should emphasize the word *shared* rather than as communicated on high for senior-level management to internal stakeholders. It may be necessary to hold special events in which the values are discussed every 5 or 10 years to examine the change brought on by social and cultural trends in relation to enterprise values and to reinvigorate employee understanding. Values and culture, however, must align with mission or purpose, strategy, and business model, all of which are subject to change based upon external factors. Often, after periods of several years, enterprises will revisit and refine their values through research among internal stakeholders, gauging knowledge of and commitment to the values, and examining the extent to which the values are still fitting and appropriate. Many organizations choose to keep the same enduring values, while other companies refine or rewrite values and mission statements at this point. However, sustaining involves a process of aligning the enterprise's core ethical values with the inclusion of these values at all levels.

Sustaining ethics over time means not only routine inclusion and discussion of core values, but also reinvigorating them through training seminars, internal communications initiatives, CEO forums, and so on. Efforts to highlight the essential role of core values in the enterprise culture should be highlighted so that they are not assumed, irrelevant, or forgotten. In order to sustain them, core values must be enlivened and acted upon every day (Men and Bowen 2017). In that manner, the enterprise has truly achieved a distinctive character that provides continuity across changing leadership, stability for internal stakeholders, aligns with the expectations of external stakeholders, and offers consistency over time. Such an enterprise character can offer a competitive advantage in the marketplace by building ongoing relationships with stakeholders.

Summary

A strong enterprise corporate character should be purposefully built. Knowing an enterprise's identity based on its core values, mission, and vision is vital. Corporate culture has a character separate from the individuals who comprise it. A participative culture that builds ethical values, discussion, understanding, support, and action is a crucial component of building character. The CCO plays an essential role in orienting, institutionalizing, and sustaining that character, as well as acting as an ethical conscience of the enterprise and ethics counsel. The USAA and Southwest Airlines cases provide innovative examples of how companies build and sustain their character.

CHAPTER 5

Stakeholder Engagement— Creating and Sustaining Advocacy

Michael Fernandez, Matthew Gonring, and Sally Benjamin Young

This chapter provides a case-based understanding of stakeholder engagement as a strategic, organized, and structured approach to managing relationships with key constituencies that can influence enterprise business. A stakeholder is a particular individual or group of individuals who influence or are influenced by the enterprise. As such, stakeholders may be customers, employees, stockholders, investors, and governmental and nongovernmental organizations (Michaelson and Stacks 2017).

Stakeholder Engagement is an emerging strategic role played by the public relations/corporate communication function in managing environments, processes, relationships, and methodologies in which enterprises operate. This chapter includes an analysis of pharmaceutical company Lundbeck's dealings with stakeholders regarding uses of its former drug pentobarbital, along with the findings from a 2014 report by the Arthur W. Page Society titled, *Authentic Advocacy: How Five Leading Companies are Redefining Stakeholder Engagement.*

The need for a refreshed look at stakeholder engagement is clear in the Arthur W. Page Society Report *The New CCO* released in 2016:

The Chief Communications Officer (CCO) of today is at a critical inflection point. The environment in which enterprises operate is fraught with challenges: emerging competitors reinventing traditional business models; changing demographic, regulatory, and sociopolitical conditions; new modes of work; and an ongoing paradigm shift in how individuals engage with one another and with organizations.... Evolution of the enterprise in the face of these new realities is required, and CCOs increasingly will be central to their ability to do so. (p. 5)

Any one of these factors could have a profound and lasting economic impact on the enterprise, its operations, and its policies. Taken collectively, they underscore the complexity of today's environment and the need for a more conscious and conscientious effort for engaging stakeholders with a vested interest in how the enterprise operates.

With virtually every stakeholder having access to the public stage via multiple communication channels, even small voices magnified by the power of social networks can wield influence. Long gone are the days where enterprises could operate with a degree of autonomy, making policy decisions in a vacuum or boardroom far from the ears of customers or even internal stakeholders. Enterprise graveyards are littered with examples from Enron to Lehman Brothers, whose demise was hastened in part by a failure to listen to or recognize influential stakeholders and the impact they can have on business. Today's hyper-connected and hyper-competitive global marketplace means that effectively managing stakeholder engagement has never been more important. And, in a world where the pace of change will likely only accelerate, the need to anticipate and monitor trends and interests emerging from a diverse set of global stakeholders must not be overlooked.

The power of diverse stakeholder constituencies to influence enterprise brands and reputation is heightened by the fact that many stakeholders *want* to influence how brands and organizations operate on issues they care about. In the global marketplace, issues of prominence that might previously have been confined to a local market can go viral overnight, having far reaching and dramatic political, social, economic, and ethical consequences. This has prompted many enterprises to become more transparent, with many reporting more information about their operations relative to their environmental and social impact. Even some privately held enterprises have commenced reporting quarterly earnings, even though such reporting is not required by any legal entity.

Until relatively recently, many enterprises concentrated primarily on inner circle stakeholders (customers, employees, investors), investing little time and effort in building broader relationships. Enterprise communication traditionally focused mainly on the media and easily identifiable key influencers.

While there is broad acknowledgement today that business should be engaged with external stakeholders, this has not always been so. Historically, there were starts and stops to broader corporate engagement, notably in the late 19th and early 20th centuries as populist and progressive responses to the "gilded age" prompted community chests (which became the United Way), philanthropies, and nonprofits to form with corporate support. In the post-World War II era through the 1960s when civic action on behalf of civil rights, the environment, and the equality for women changed government policies and promoted enterprises to create diversity initiatives and health, safety, and environment initiatives coupled with broader community engagement. But for most of the 20th century the view forwarded by Adolf Berle (1931) in the *Harvard Law Review* that business should be solely focused on shareholders is what prevailed. In the wake of the 1960s, one of the founders of Hewlett-Packard, David Packard, argued that business had a responsibility to make "a contribution to society"; and the Research Institute at his alma mater, Stanford University, in 1963, was among the first to define "stakeholders."[1] But by 1970, conservative economist Friedman (1984) was arguing that the only responsibility of business was to make a profit, and Jack Welch of General Electric in 1981 was arguing for a focus on shareholder value (1981), a concept that dominated the business thinking of the 1980s. During that decade, though, Darden Professor Edward Freeman (Freeman and Reed 1984) articulated the merits of a broad stakeholder approach. Through it all, an unwritten social contract emerged that essentially held that business could meet its obligations to society if it produced quality products and services at reasonable prices, provided steady employment in a healthy and safe environment, and offered reasonable support for community institutions.

Toward the end of the 20th century and early in the 21st, that social contract was threatened by multiple forces—the perceived greed of business leaders and shareowners as leveraged buyouts, layoffs, and dramatic reductions in employee benefits became commonplace; the malfeasance

---

[1] As quoted in Freeman, R.E. 1984. *Strategic Management: A Stakeholder Approach*. Freeman is particularly known for his work on stakeholder theory.

of the Enron/WorldCom era, during which a number of corporate leaders were incarcerated; and the dramatic breakdown of trust in business during the global financial meltdown in 2008 that led to the Great Recession.

During the same period, responsible enterprises were exploring corporate social responsibility, actively engaging their workforce, and establishing concerted philanthropic and sustainability efforts. Nongovernmental organizations (NGOs) were becoming more assertive and adversarial in opposing corporate policies, and social media made it possible to access information more easily, organize people with similar interests to form connections, and unite them to advocate for change.

These developments hastened the drive for greater transparency. In 1997 the Global Reporting Initiative (GRI and CDP n.d.) was launched out of Boston with the intent to have a comparative reporting tool for enterprises to share metrics and status relative to their impact on the environment, health, and society. In 2000, the Carbon Disclosure Project (CDP) was established in the United Kingdom to assess how business was impacting global climate change. By 2015, 7,500 organizations were using the GRI guidelines, and more than 5,500 companies across the globe were supplying data and metrics to the CDP.

These reporting projects illustrate the dynamic new environment of stakeholder engagement captured in the 2007 Page Society report, *The Authentic Enterprise*: "In addition to the familiar constituencies with which corporations have interacted in the past, there is now a diverse array of communities, interests, nongovernmental organizations and individuals—all far more able to collaborate…around shared interests and…reach large audiences" (p. 12).

An implicit license to operate or a social contract that an enterprise must meet to be sanctioned to operate with various societal stakeholders has never been more relevant and simply reinforces the wisdom of Arthur W. Page that, "All business in a democratic society begins with public permission and exists by public approval" (http://awpagesociety.com/site/historical-perspective).

Stakeholder Engagement Defined

A stakeholder is defined *as any constituent who has a "stake" or interest in the activities of an enterprise.* As noted, traditional key stakeholders for public enterprises are employees, shareholders, and customers (http://investipedia.com/terms/s/stakeholder.asp n.d.). Today, practicing communication executives often define stakeholders far more broadly (McCarthy 2016) including bankers, suppliers, prospective employees, communities where one operates or seeks to operate, governments, consumers—as distinguished from business-to-business customers, NGOs or "civil society," and intergovernmental organizations (IGOs) such as the World Bank and the International Monetary Fund (IMF). Professional communicators often include the media and depending on context may qualify media as a distribution channel to reach stakeholders.

In Neil Jeffrey's 2009 report from the Cranfield University School of Management, he points out,

> Stakeholder Engagement is crucially different to stakeholder management: stakeholder engagement implies a willingness to listen; to discuss issues of interest to stakeholders of the organization; and, critically, the organization has to be prepared to consider changing what it aims to achieve and how it operates, as a result of stakeholder engagement. (p. 380)

In fact, channels of communication and stakeholder groups are so broad and sophisticated that they are beyond management, thereby requiring more thoughtful engagement. Dialogue and monitoring then become key tools with which enterprises seek to influence and understand perceptions and behaviors.

The logic of stakeholder engagement is that stakeholders have the ability to influence the enterprise's success and the decisions that underlie them. Jeffrey's (2009) report in many ways underscores the two-way symmetrical public relations model envisioned by Professor James E. Grunig and Todd Hunt in 1984, which holds that organizations use research and dialogue to negotiate with publics, resolve conflicts, and promote mutual understanding and respect.

Deloitte's *2008 AccountAbility 1000 Stakeholder Engagement Standard* (p. 2) report defines stakeholders as "…groups who affect and/or could be affected by an organization's activities, products, or services and associated performance."

Approaches to stakeholder engagement will continue to evolve as new technologies, globalization, and other forces further transform the way organizations operate and engage. As the enterprise moves from "talking at and monitoring" and closer to "partnering with" stakeholders, the nature and dynamic of the relationships are shifting toward one of cooperation, collaboration, and, importantly, interdependency. This has also prompted a shift in enterprise orientation from *issues management* to *relationship management* where enterprises work with foes and friends alike and impacting how trust is won or lost.

Functional Development from Channel Owner to Problem Solver, Business Leader, and Collaborator

The professional practice of public relations/corporate communication is shifting away from the traditional functional one-way communication directed to specific stakeholders. According to that same Deloitte 2008 report, with the rise of social media, and stakeholders having equal access to the same technology and becoming influencers in channels, corporate communication professionals are bringing external information and dialogue inside the enterprise, as well as developing new, sophisticated approaches to issues management, stakeholder engagement, and thought leadership. Today's CCO is not just a communicator; he or she is a problem solver and relationship builder using the latest technologies and communication channels to both better understand and connect with stakeholders.

According to the USC Annenberg *2016 Global Communications Report* less than one-third of the average enterprise corporate communication department's media budget is being spent on earned media—the traditional focus for corporate communication. Slightly more is being spent on owned media, such as websites and blogs.[2] It projects that, by 2020, slightly more than a quarter of media budgets will be focused

---

[2] Earned media is that which the enterprise has received when its actions are reported in the media by "reporters" who often receive leads from the enterprise's media relations department. Owned media, such as websites and YouTube videos, are created and transmitted by the enterprise. While both are more aligned with push information (from enterprise to stakeholder), social media is a push–pull strategy that operates on what was earlier defined as *two-way symmetric communication*—or the establishment of a dialogue in which either the enterprise or the stakeholder can initiate the communication and/or respond to a social media communication.

on earned channels. This trend toward a balance of earned, owned, and social media recognizes that effective stakeholder engagement requires a balanced approach along with investments in digital-based programming.

The 2016 Page Society report *The New CCO* cited technological and demographic changes affecting the functional development of managing stakeholder relations. The report indicated that enterprises have become a builder of social value and a partner with governments and NGOs.

Increasingly, stakeholders, including consumers, activists, even some investors, and the general public, expect business not only to act responsibly but to actually solve global problems and create social value.

Changing expectations of business and the enterprise demands a more direct approach to engagement with stakeholders as the following case from Lundbeck illustrates.

Case: Lundbeck's Collaborative Dialogue Helps Address Complex Challenges

Having one's thinking challenged by stakeholders with a different perspective than your own frequently expands the initial thinking of what's possible, pressing a search for alternatives that might never have been explored, and ultimately driving outcomes never thought possible. That was the case for Lundbeck when the company learned, much to its surprise, that in January 2011 one of its medicines had been co-opted by American prisons for lethal injections used in capital punishment.

Pentobarbital was part of the company's portfolio of epilepsy therapies used to treat a serious and life-threatening emergency epilepsy, called status epilepticus—the cause of approximately 42,000 deaths a year in the United States.[3] But when a previously used drug in lethal injections became unavailable, prisons began turning to pentobarbital

---

[3] The company announced the divestiture of this product, along with a host of other noncore products, on 12/22/2011—after having effectively resolved the controversy surrounding the drug use in prisons.

as a replacement in the lethal cocktail administered to prisoners on death row, overnight thrusting Lundbeck into the debate on capital punishment. Withdrawing the product from the market was not in the best interest of patients who needed it for emergency use, yet misuse of this product was generating intense criticism of Lundbeck.

Meaningful Stakeholder Engagement Begins with Corporate Character

Lundbeck adamantly opposed the use of its drug for executions because ending lives contradicts everything the company is in business to do: provide therapies that improve people's lives. Patients are at the center of everything Lundbeck does—defining its purpose and driving its behaviors. Enterprise leaders ensure that its character resonates with every employee by encouraging them to focus on the individuals behind the disease, engage with patients directly, and understand their specific needs. This personal connection not only reinforces the relationship it has with patients, but also contributes to better company decision making.

While deploying pentobarbital for lethal injection was in direct conflict with its core beliefs, Lundbeck had to assess what means it had to prevent this unexpected use. Once a drug is approved in the United States, nothing prevents physicians from using it as they deem appropriate, though Lundbeck expects its products to be used in a safe and appropriate manner. Moreover, to Lundbeck's knowledge no pharmaceutical company had ever succeeded in thwarting a prison's use of drugs in lethal injection, which remains legal in 34 states.

That said, the use of its drug by prisons was deeply problematic for Lundbeck from an enterprise corporate character standpoint (see Chapter 4) and a human rights perspective. The Lundbeck case highlighted a vexing dilemma: how to prevent a nonmedical use it did not condone while preserving access to the medicine for those patients who needed it.

Building Shared Belief

Almost immediately, Lundbeck was contacted by Reprieve, a legal action charity that works to prevent the misuse of medicines in executions. Reprieve asked Lundbeck to stop the flow of the drug to prisons. While Reprieve and Lundbeck were in full agreement on this point, there was lack of alignment about how this could be achieved. Nevertheless, actions matter. Lundbeck needed to find a way to simultaneously uphold its commitments to patients and to society—and for its stakeholders to understand the importance of keeping the needs of patients at the forefront of its decisions. Lundbeck brought its case straight to the states using or considering the use of pentobarbital for lethal injection, writing letters to Governors and departments of correction to urge them to discontinue this use. Those pleas fell short of changing the outcome.

Aligning Decision Making with Corporate Character

Despite having no clear path forward, Lundbeck continued to engage in a constructive dialogue with human rights advocates to discuss and evaluate ideas to prevent prison use. Not only was Reprieve asking the company for a solution but activist investors, European policy makers, other NGOs, individuals, and even its own employees, especially in Europe, asked the company to do more. Soon there were calls for Lundbeck to withdraw its product from the market. Yet, what seemed obvious to these stakeholders contradicted Lundbeck's principles. While withdrawing the product from the market appeared easy from a business perspective—the product represented only about 1 percent of global sales— it would have been unethical and a tragedy for patients who needed this important therapy.

Even Danish physicians questioned the need to treat status epilepticus[4] with pentobarbital because Danish medical practice differed from that in the United States. In order to gain an objective view on the medical need for pentobarbital in the United States, Lundbeck commissioned two leading independent research firms to field a blinded

---

[4] Status epilepticus (SE) is a medical emergency associated with significant morbidity and mortality. SE is defined as a continuous seizure lasting more than 30 minutes, or two or more seizures without full recovery of consciousness between any of them (Cherian and Thomas 2009).

survey of more than 200 hospitals and physicians that validated the importance of this therapy in medical practice. Ninety percent of the respondents stated that options for treating patients requiring emergency control of certain acute convulsive episodes would be compromised if pentobarbital were no longer available. Furthermore, 95 percent reported that it is very important for their institution to have continued access to pentobarbital for potential use in patient care. All survey respondents were from academic institutions, large community hospitals or epilepsy centers in the United States.

Further dialogue with medical experts reinforced the survey data. One U.S. epilepsy thought leader stated:

> Pentobarbital is the ultimate gold standard in North America for controlling seizures in patients with refractory status epilepticus when other medications fail…if pentobarbital were not available, many patients would suffer, likely having additional brain damage from uncontrolled seizures, and possible higher mortality. (Hirsch April 29, 2011)

Another noted that "There is no equivalent barbiturate…limiting or discontinuing the supply [of pentobarbital] could have a significant negative effect on patient care" (Frost March 25, 2011). With the importance of this medical therapy confirmed, Lundbeck faced the challenge of addressing how to sustain access for physicians and their patients to this life-saving medical treatment while ensuring it could not be used in executions.

Action

Continuing Dialogue to Find the Most Effective Solution

Lundbeck explored a broad range of potential remedies to restrict access by prisons, involving bodies such as the U.S. Food and Drug Administration, the wholesalers to whom Lundbeck directly sold the drug and who are then responsible for selling to end users, and physician associations to find the least disruptive way to ensure appropriate use of pentobarbital. None of these avenues proved effective. Still, stakeholders from Reprieve and other human rights organizations, relevant government officials, health authorities, and third-party experts all lobbied Lundbeck to go further, leading it to test its long-held assumptions about how to manage its supply chain.

Lundbeck announced in July 2011 that it would no longer sell pentobarbital through its wholesalers. Instead, it adopted a restricted distribution "drop ship" program based on a binding agreement with distributers of the product that it would only be sold to legitimate medical customers. Under this program, hospital customers would need to sign a form stating that the purchase of pentobarbital was for their own use and would not be used for lethal injection. After appropriate paperwork was completed, the product would be sent directly to the customer. This solution required collaboration across Lundbeck to brainstorm how this system could work, gather the appropriate data needed, modify systems and processes, and drive implementation of a complex, but necessary program.

Advocacy

Access Preserved and Misuse Prevented

Lundbeck's new system was hugely successful. While pentobarbital remained available for patient care, prisons started reporting shortages. Reprieve began pointing to Lundbeck as an example of how pharmaceutical companies could cut off supply of their products to prisons. Praising Lundbeck's intense effort, Maya Foia of Reprieve said,

> Lundbeck's action has changed the landscape of corporate social responsibility in the pharmaceutical industry. Many pharmaceutical companies lament the use of their medicines in executions—Lundbeck didn't just lament it, they took active steps to prevent it. In doing so, the company proved that pharmaceutical manufacturers don't have to be complicit in capital punishment; they have a choice as to whether they

facilitate executions by supplying prisons with lethal injection drugs. In short, they were true to the values of their profession (Reprieve 2012).

Amnesty Denmark tweeted, "#DeathPenalty in the USA is in decline as states wrestle to find drugs for lethal injections usat.ly/1k-G5WKJ @LundbeckUS."

Lundbeck remains a leader on the misuse of medicines in executions. It was the first manufacturer to sign the *Pharmaceutical Hippocratic Oath*, signaling its commitment to making medicines for the health and benefit of mankind. Lundbeck also became the first recipient of Reprieve's new *Corporate Social Responsibility Award for Ethical Leadership in the Pharmaceutical Industry*, in recognition of the steps the company took to prevent the use of its medicines in executions in the United States.

Analysis

As noted in the Arthur W. Page Society's (2013b) report on *The CEO View: The Impact of Communications on Corporate Character in a 24×7 Digital World*: "Adversity can be a chance to articulate and reinforce for all stakeholders the company's values at a time when unusual attention is focused on them" (p. 16). Difficult as the pentobarbital situation proved to be for Lundbeck, its innovative solution presented an opportunity for it to demonstrate its unwavering commitment to patients.

Drawing on a commitment to transparency and authenticity, including its responsiveness to media inquiries and continuous public updates on its efforts, Lundbeck persevered in developing a unique solution to a global problem that has since been replicated by other drug manufacturers. It could have divested the product without having a tested solution in place to avoid the challenges of controlling the use of its product in a free market. But its commitment to focusing on the *person* behind the disease served as its moral compass, as noted in Chapter 4. No patient facing the dangers of status epilepticus would be left behind.

By collaborating with its stakeholders, Lundbeck blazed a trail to impose restrictions on distribution, reinforcing that there is always a way to do the right thing. Six months later and only after ensuring that its restricted distribution program to prevent misuse would continue to be effective over the long term, the company divested pentobarbital and contractually obligated the buyer to continue the process that remains in effect today.

Findings

An analysis of the Lundbeck case provides nine related insights regarding an enterprise's corporate character. Further, six additional action steps were identified as important to establishing enterprise authentic engagement with its stakeholder constituencies.

The Fundamental Importance of Corporate Character

One of the more intriguing learnings from the case suggests that enterprise corporate character is, indeed, at the heart of effective stakeholder engagement.

Finding 1: Clear, Compelling Character Promotes Belief and Engagement

Although enterprises express their corporate character in various ways, many regularly review, update, and/or revalidate their identity, beliefs, values, and/or purpose statements. Avoiding corporate and business jargon, the companies favor language that is clear, concrete, specific, memorable, and even inspiring.

As a mission-driven organization, Lundbeck has given extensive thought to its corporate character. Lundbeck is driven by its patient-driven purpose and dedication to those it serves—people suffering from psychiatric and neurological disorders. The company is guided by three principals: *focus* (on innovation in four key areas of brain disorders while creating value for all our stakeholders), *passion* (to help patients and communities the company serves), and *being responsible* (demonstrating respect, open-mindedness, and integrity).

Lundbeck, 70 percent owned by a foundation that contributes nearly $100 million annually to scientific research, could have made science the centerpiece of its enterprise corporate culture expressions. But with insights first discovered by the communication team in its U.S. operations, the company chose a more humanistic approach that oriented employees toward patients and their families.

For Lundbeck, the words at the heart of its culture statement ring clear and true, making it easy for stakeholders to grasp enterprise intent and for employees to consistently demonstrate behaviors and design experiences that engender customer trust.

Finding 2: Broader Span of Control Aligns Culture and Intensifies Engagement

Functions with a broader span of control and/or influence are better positioned to concentrate enterprise attention and resources on common stakeholder engagement strategies and tactics. Such enterprises use organizational structure and disciplined collaboration processes to align their corporate culture with behavior, thereby enhancing relationships with crucial stakeholders.

Finding 3: Corporate Character Shapes Business Outcomes

Lundbeck's expansion from a rare-disease-focused American neurology business to therapy areas involving significantly larger patient populations facing diseases like depression, schizophrenia, and Alzheimer's and Parkinson's diseases required a major expansion of its workforce. Using the platform of a clear and compelling culture, Lundbeck knew it could swiftly integrate new recruits, create belief, and drive advocacy. Lundbeck's vice president of public affairs, Sally Benjamin Young, believes understanding and working within the framework of corporate culture is "not just a nice thing to do, but a way to drive strategic focus and business success."

Finding 4: Stakeholder Engagement Today Is a Rigorous, Disciplined, and Data-Driven Process

Thanks to greater access to information, high levels of transparency, and other forces, stakeholder engagement is now a more rigorous, systematic, and data-driven discipline.

Finding 5: Employees Can Be a Company's Best Resource for Building Belief with External Stakeholders

An "inside-out" approach to engagement has helped some enterprises turn employees into a potent resource in gaining the trust and support of external stakeholder constituencies. At Lundbeck, employees take enormous pride in their work. This is particularly evident in their close personal engagement in patient communities. Young notes, "These stakeholders—patients and their families, physicians and nurses—need to know that you care before they care about what you know." Lundbeck's Starfish Story (http://lundbeck.com/us/our-commitment/community-involvement/your-partner-in-epilepsy), a parable about a boy questioned about the impact of saving a single starfish that washed up on a beach when there are so many to save, resonates with employees whose mantra is "making a difference, one patient at a time." The story is part of a broader "We are Lundbeck" campaign that focuses on seeing the person behind the disease by putting real patients front and center in a wide range of initiatives and communications. From efforts like these, many Lundbeck employees get to know patients and their families personally, learning about their needs and what it means to live with their diseases. This empathetic perspective and personal connection contribute to better corporate decision making, Young says.

Finding 6: Partnerships Are the Basis for Sustained Belief and Engagement

Most enterprises concur that corporate philanthropy continues to play a role in building stakeholder belief and advocacy. They believe close, long-term, two-way partnerships are quickly becoming the more valuable currency in establishing trust and activating advocates. Lundbeck's approach is illustrative. A few years ago, it realized that the norm for pharmaceutical companies—underwriting research, events, conferences, and the like—had its limits. The approach was largely transactional, derided by some as checkbook philanthropy or worse. While financial support is needed, Lundbeck's investment of time was equally critical. As a smaller and younger enterprise in the United States, Lundbeck saw an opportunity to extend its reach and impact on patients by forging close, long-term engagements with patient organizations across all of its disease areas in epilepsy, mental health, Alzheimer's, and Parkinson's disease.

Lundbeck's approach started with a listening ear, not a corporate check. Executives consistently meet with patient groups to review their existing needs and future priorities, collaborate on various initiatives, and to conduct programs in communities to help patients and their families. One initiative led to others, earning Lundbeck a reputation among patients, doctors, and others in the health care community as actively supporting and engaging with patient communities, and genuinely caring about making a tangible difference.

One illustration of this is PatientView's (2016) 2015 Corporate Reputation of Pharma study, which reflects the views of 106 American patient organizations and about 28 pharmaceutical companies. Lundbeck in the United States not only ranked first in overall corporate reputation and first on all six attributes (patient-centricity, information, patient safety, usefulness of products, transparency, and integrity), but according to the report, "the percentages awarded Lundbeck by U.S. patient groups stand among the highest ever recorded in PatientView's Corporate Reputation surveys" (p. 46). By building shared belief with patient advocacy organizations, Lundbeck has seen stakeholders take concrete actions—from advocating policy change at the state and federal level, to advancing research, even driving change within communities to benefit patients.

Finding 7: Advocacy at Scale Is Relative

When the Page Society released its volume on corporate character, *Building Belief: A New Model for Activating Corporate Character and Authentic Advocacy* (2012a), some members found the idea of advocacy at scale a bit daunting. However, *scale is relative*. Scale is not always large numbers of likes, follows, hits, letters, or phone calls from stakeholders—though volume can get results. Rather, it is about deep, mutually beneficial relationships that allow the enterprise and its stakeholders to achieve their respective goals over the long term.

Lundbeck's interactions with its patient communities help establish Lundbeck as a trusted partner. This trust is both a significant source of pride and a serious responsibility that guides everything the Lundbeck team does. As is illustrated by this example, scale is relative to the issues at hand and the business and stakeholder impact.

Finding 8: Engaged Stakeholders Can Help Companies Mitigate Business Risks and Identify New Business Opportunities

Partnerships with patient organizations help Lundbeck monitor the pulse of emerging issues and needs that impact the patient communities affected by its disease areas.

Finding 9: It Is Essential to Sustain Stakeholder Engagement

Leadership and Ownership Matter

Young (2016) observed that even in enterprises like Lundbeck, where collaboration is exalted, colleagues in other functions are not sitting around waiting for the CCO to curate corporate culture and drive stakeholder engagement. Rather, the commitment to patients is so deeply embedded that employees across Lundbeck participate in patient events even on weekends and evenings. Stated simply, *stakeholder engagement is an enterprisewide accountability.*

Seven Action Steps for Enterprises to Build Authentic Engagement

1. *As a prerequisite to building strong stakeholder relationships, build a strong corporate character.* Being authentically worthy of trust is a necessary prerequisite to building trust among stakeholders. The New Model for Enterprise Communication articulated in *Building Belief* is clear about the relationship between deserving trust by having a strong corporate character and building trust through authentic stakeholder engagement. To be effective this must be more than a collection of words labeled as "credo," "purpose," or "vision," it must be backed by consistent actions and behaviors across the enterprise.

2. *Using organizational structure and collaboration processes to create an enterprisewide commitment.* As derived from research and articulated in *The New CCO* (2016), the CCO must be an integrator (for more

on this, see Chapter 7). Corporate communication functions with a broader span of control and/or influence are better positioned to concentrate organizational attention and resources on common stakeholder engagement strategies and tactics. In reality, the scope of responsibility of corporate communication functions varies widely. But all CCOs and communication departments should be conscious of the need to exercise broad influence across the C-Suite to drive an enterprise-wide commitment to activating corporate character and building deep, meaningful, and lasting stakeholder relationships. CCOs today must be adept at exercising influence, whether they have specific line authority or not. As noted by Harrison and Mühlberg (2014), this requires strong peer-to-peer leadership skills and the ability to create and win support for processes that effectively marshal enterprise resources.

3. *Build a rigorous, systematic, and data-driven methodology.* Enterprises consistently address stakeholder engagement through rigorous, disciplined, systematic approaches that rely heavily on data analytics and new technology—sometimes sophisticated, sometimes simple. These approaches analyzed both stakeholders and the issues that motivate them, allowing the enterprise to lay a strong foundation for building shared belief and encouraging supportive actions.

4. *Empower and enlist employees as a resource for building belief with external stakeholders.* Enterprises have long understood that engaged employees can be their best ambassadors. But the level of engagement made possible by new social media tools, combined with a marked trend in which publics have less trust in authoritative figures, makes the power and potential of employee advocacy even more potent.

5. *Focus on developing partnerships with stakeholders, not "one-off" transactions.* True stakeholder engagement is about building relationships that last. Enterprise corporate philanthropy can play a role, but authentic relationships are two-way. That requires moving beyond transactional activities—underwriting research, sponsoring events, and the like—to long-term agreements based on shared belief and mutual commitments. Two-way partnerships (c.f., Grunig 1987) require true listening and a willingness to change to build mutual benefit. Viewing stakeholders as potential partners instead

of adversaries is a mindset that has transformed the way progressive companies approach building relationships.

6. *Recognize that scale varies depending on the nature of your enterprise, the stakeholders you work with, and the scope of the issue.* The advent of social media has changed the nature of advocacy. Today, enterprises often build shared belief with thousands or millions of people who become committed partners and feel they have a shared stake in the success of the enterprise. Today, *everyone* is an influencer. For some enterprises and issues, the interested and affected stakeholders can be much smaller. But building advocates is no less important. CCOs accustomed to using mass communication to reach large audiences sometimes need to recalibrate their approach to build shared belief and advocacy one stakeholder at a time, determining which channels to use, and gauging the level of effort for each stakeholder group and each issue. Regardless of size, nothing replaces face-to-face engagement and relationship building, which together with online outreach can enable considerable advocacy and influence at scale.

7. *Be committed for the long term.* Creating meaningful stakeholder relationships is hard work that must be sustained over time. Enterprises that do not make the long-term commitment risk at best becoming irrelevant and at worst an unreliable partner. The best enterprises marshal a steady commitment that is reflective of changes in the external environment and within stakeholder constituencies. Just as strategy and operations require sustained dedication and established processes, so too do enterprise corporate character and stakeholder engagement. Over time, approaches will evolve as the enterprise learns and grows, but what must never change is the commitment to invest the energy of the enterprise in building relationships that matter—to help solve problems, provide an outside-in perspective, and confer an implicit license to operate.

Summary

While CCOs can and must take a leadership role, they also recognize that, when their peers work with them to own stakeholder relationships, the entire organization benefits. Leading the way in the important area of building culture requires the maturity to share ownership and involve everyone necessary in the process and share credit for success.

In a massive global enterprise, stakeholder engagement is dispersed across business units, functions, and geographies. There may be 50 to 100 employees in a given business unit with some responsibility for stakeholder relationships, and, increasingly, a significant percentage of a country manager's time may be devoted to stakeholder engagement and social risk management. That is why some enterprises are developing corporate centers of excellence to ensure global consistency across business, functions, and geographies. It is also why several of these are using extensive training, development, and people management tools, including job rotations and succession planning, to ensure coverage and retain institutional knowledge in effective stakeholder management.

Communicating aspects of culture and engaging stakeholders are two sides of the same coin. In today's increasingly volatile world, both must be present to assure value.

CHAPTER 6

The Changing and Expanding Foundational Role of the CCO

Charlotte R. Otto, Gary Sheffer, and Donald K. Wright

Amidst the transformational shifts impacting the communication function, the foundational role of the chief communication officer (CCO) is more important than ever. As established in the Arthur W. Page Society report, *The New CCO: Transforming Enterprises in a Changing World* (2016), the CCO has become not only a central actor in leading an enterprise's stakeholder engagement and reputation management efforts, but also a leader in building corporate character and shaping enterprisewide strategies. The CCO's broad and integrated view of the enterprise, communication, and external landscape is becoming increasingly vital.

The New CCO distills the foundational role into three key areas:

1. *Strategic business leader and counselor*—this requires the CCO to interpret and act upon changes in the external environment, based on insights from key stakeholder relationships, data analytics, and other sources, to lead and influence enterprise direction. As a result, today's CCO must have deeper business and enterprise understanding, a broader network of strategic relationships, and new tools to stay ahead of trends and inform business decision making.

2. *Steward of enterprise reputation*—the CCO remains a critical "conscience counselor" to ensure the enterprise's actions are consistent with its most deeply held beliefs—its character. This requires even earlier and deeper integration into business decisions and the

enterprise risk management system. It also requires seamless collaboration with enterprise brand-building efforts.

3. *Effective communicator*—the CCO must lead sophisticated, coordinated communication, based on strategic business insight, enterprise
   culture, and external understanding to effectively execute strategy
   to deliver enterprise goals. As communication tactics transform,
   the CCO must bring sharper expertise in modern storytelling, new
   media, and data-based measurement tools, and be able to adapt
   approaches globally.

In addition to these foundational elements, the CCO retains the
enduring role of building an agile, sustainable organization and attracting
and developing the best communication talent. The CCO has particular accountability to ensure stakeholder diversity is incorporated into the
enterprise and that diversity of thought and style are leveraged to drive
better ideas.

While the central elements of the CCO's foundational role are
not new, the changing business and communication environment has
intensified its importance and expanded how this role is delivered (see
Chapter 9). This is the focus of this chapter.

The Evolution of the Foundational CCO Role

Two of the first CCOs for major enterprises shaped the foundational role
of the CCO. The elements of strategic business leader and counselor,
steward of enterprise reputation, and effective communicator were central
to how they defined their jobs. These pioneering CCOs are Paul Garrett
of General Motors and Arthur W. Page of AT&T.

Paul Garrett worked more than a decade in journalism—including
a long stint as business editor for the *New York Evening Post*—before he
was hired by General Motors in 1931 as the company's first public relations director. Garrett's charge from GM's Chairman Alfred P. Sloan, Jr.,
was to "interpret the corporation to the public and, in turn to help (Sloan)
try to understand what the country was thinking" (Golden 1967, p. 62).

Garrett spent 25 years at GM and made certain public relations played
a significant role at the policy stage of decision making. He insisted GM's

programs and actions supported its policy. By 1939 his staff numbered more than 50 and his budget exceeded $2 million (Henige 1993), both significant for the time. Noted public relations historian Scott M. Cutlip (1995) praised Garrett for building an innovative program that was widely copied by other corporations.

Arthur W. Page was Vice President of AT&T from 1927 until 1946. Griese (2001) claims many consider Page to have been the most influential corporate public relations practitioner of the 20th Century. He worked 22 years at Doubleday before joining the world's largest telephone company and becoming the first corporate officer responsible for public relations at a major enterprise. A Harvard University graduate, Page enthusiastically accepted the offer from AT&T Chairman and CEO Walter Gifford when it became clear his would be a policy-making position. Page was elected to AT&T's board of directors in 1931 and remained a director until 1948.

Block (2004) points out that Page's imprint extends well beyond AT&T because he served on boards of directors of several other businesses and was a member of Harvard's board of overseers. Page advocated telling the truth, listening to the customer, managing for tomorrow, and conducting public relations as if the entire company depended upon it, values that were later codified into the Page Principles by the founders of the Page Society.

In 1983, the Arthur W. Page Society was created for enterprise corporate communication officers, public relations agency leaders, and educators who seek to enrich and strengthen the role of the chief communications officer. Now in its fourth decade, the Page Society facilitates discussions, networking, and programs designed to advance the policy-making role of CCOs based on the founding members' creation of the "Page Principles" based on a review of his spoken and written comments on the role of corporate communication in the enterprise (http://awpagesociety.com/site/the-page-principles and more on its history at: http://awpagesociety.com/site/historical-perspective). Burson (2013), the founding chairman of Burson-Marsteller, has described how public relations has evolved during the eight decades he has been involved in the industry. When he entered the business at the end of World War II, Burson says clients hired public relations people to help answer the question, "How should we say it?" Decisions about what to do, how to do it, and even what to say were made by others. Burson observed that over time public relations people worked their way up the ladder of organizational influence to a point where most of today's successful enterprises have public relations experts advising them about what to do, how to do it, what to say, *and* how to say it.

Cutlip (Cutlip and Center 1971) has pointed out that the role of the CCO branched out from that of a defensive communicator and order-taker to that of a valued member of the management team including a seat at the enterprise's decision-making table. By the 2000s, the CCO had become firmly embedded in most companies—but the scope of responsibility and influence still varied from enterprise to enterprise.

Although the role of the CCO and the corporate communication function was impressive and involved plenty of two-way communication within GM, AT&T, and a few other enterprises, it is important to note the growth and importance of the communication function and the CCO progressed differently within many enterprises. While there were some that treated communication as a truly senior-level managerial function, there were others where communication involved not much more than publicity.

The Increasingly Important CCO Role

Over the past decade, the role of the CCO has increased dramatically and has become even more important to enterprise success. A positive reputation has always been a central element of sustained business success, and the CCO is the chief minder of reputation and the driving force behind building and protecting it. Yet in this era of hyper-connectivity, radical transparency, and stakeholder activism, it is harder to build and protect reputation, thus the CCO's role is more critical and more challenging.

Stakeholder interests must be more carefully considered in business strategy and decision making. Building stakeholder relationships is more complex than ever. Through social media, employees can organize, consumers can critique, citizens can report, and activists can mobilize coordinated advocacy. With multiple channels and voices, it is harder than ever to effectively communicate the enterprise's story.

Managing these new realities requires a CCO who is a strong leader in ensuring that an enterprise's actions match its intentions and its message, that it behaves responsibly and openly, and that it is responsive to the interests of *all* stakeholders, both internal and external to the enterprise. In essence, *this is the foundational role of the "New" CCO.*

Strategic Business Leader and Counselor

CCOs have a uniquely broad view of the enterprise and its environment—from customers, to marketplace competition, to the media, to policy discussions, to shifting social priorities, to reputation vulnerabilities, and all of this across geographies. With this sweeping vantage point, enterprise leaders expect CCOs to help identify, interpret, and act upon changes in the external environment; stay steps ahead of events by monitoring traditional and social media; engage with regulators, policy makers, international governmental organizations (IGOs), and nongovernmental organizations (NGOs); and build meaningful, trusting, and lasting relationships with stakeholders rooted in a genuine understanding of their interests.

In an informal poll of senior communications executives conducted as part of *The New CCO*, 92 percent said that CEOs rely on CCOs for their thinking to a greater degree today than in the past (Arthur W. Page Society 2016). Former GE CEO Jack Welch said at a recent Page Society event that the CEO–CCO relationship is the most important and closest in the C-Suite.

The new leadership mandate impacting the foundational role of the CCO is to more proactively translate this broad view into insightful, impactful business counsel, and direction. This requires deeper knowledge of the business or enterprise. This can come from experiences outside traditional communication duties, as well as close collaboration and integration with business leaders and their teams. It also requires a broader and more strategic network of influential relationships with key stakeholder constituencies, as well as new tools. New analytical and monitoring techniques help track traditional and social media to identify trends, stay ahead of events, and quickly identify implications and actions (see Chapter 8).

According to Chevron CCO Dave Samson, Chevron is one company that is taking advantage of emerging technologies, new platforms, and its access to increased volumes of data to create real-time, actionable intelligence. As a result, Chevron has enhanced its ability to predict stakeholder actions, as well as business threats and opportunities.

These new capabilities are playing a central role in the energy giant's stakeholder engagement strategies, including its interactions with stakeholders most critical to advancing its business interests. Stakeholder mapping tools such as Chevron's can help provide a data-based approach to identifying the most important relationships through "big data" sets and analytics.

Sidebar: Partnership with the CEO and Senior Leaders

Support from the CEO and other members of the executive team (C-Suite) is essential to the CCO's influence as a strategic business leader and counselor regarding business decisions. Indeed, an important component of the job of any CCO must be cultivating these leaders as champions for the essential nature of effective communication and stakeholder relationships in business success. Beyond the *traditional* CCO role of message practice, media tracking, and communication training, the *new* CCO has the important role of strategic business counselor with involvement in the strategic business decisions of the C-Suite. The CCO also must develop and activate the CEO and other senior leaders as key storytellers (c.f., Harrison and Mühlberg 2014).

The relationship between successful business leaders is built on constant interaction. At the Ford Motor Company, for example, former CCO Ray Day led a team that was embedded within each function and business unit—allowing them to be always aligned with and connected to the business.

In addition, Day and the Ford Communication team conducted continual outreach to keep senior leaders "on message" and aligned with the Ford story. Global communication risks and opportunities, for example, were shared in the company's weekly business plan review meetings. Key topical messages distributed to every senior leader in the company worldwide via a weekly "Issues & Answers" document. Upcoming news-making stories were summarized in a "Ford: The Week Ahead" roundup.

Executives and subject matter experts throughout the company are engaged in media training—including periodic refreshers—to develop their own storytelling capabilities. The Ford Communication team also conducted "alignment sessions" to review messaging and expected questions ahead of every major news-making event. This all resulted in vital partnership between business leaders and Communication, fostered by strong CCO leadership.

Steward of Enterprise Reputation

The Page Model of Enterprise Communication, put forth in the Society's 2012 *Building Belief* (2012a) report, clearly illustrates that defining and activating an enterprise's corporate character is an essential prerequisite to earning public trust that generates the social license to operate (see Chapter 4). A half of the CCO's fundamental responsibility is as the steward of enterprise reputation. The second half focuses on strategic decisions regarding a focus on trust, corporate character, and stakeholder engagement with the outcome an actual engagement with stakeholders to earn that trust. It requires the CCO to ensure that the enterprise's actions match its rhetoric; that values are practiced, not merely preached; and that it is behaving responsibly, transparently, and with the interests of all stakeholders in mind. This role has long been linked to acting as an enterprise "conscience counselor" to protect long-term reputation.

As reputation stewards in today's ultratransparent, "social" world the CCO must be more deeply involved in anticipating and preventing reputation-damaging actions and issues and engaging stakeholders to build a two-way communication system that listens as well as talks. This requires even earlier and deeper influence on business decisions and central engagement in the enterprise's risk management system. Data-based assessments of reputational risk using new analytics, as well as continual organizational preparedness to respond quickly to events, now have higher priority.

Case: Reputation Stewardship

Voya Financial CCO Paul Gennaro says, "the option not to be fully transparent has disappeared and is non-existent today." He put this belief into practice in 2011 in his previous role at construction industry leader AECOM, when a potential reputation crisis arose related to a project in Libya. At the time, the United States had normalized relations with Libya and AECOM was managing a project with the Libyan government to advance public infrastructure.

As part of the project, AECOM agreed to a short-term educational internship for Khamis Gaddafi, the son of Libyan dictator Muammar Gaddafi. The internship included a trip for Khamis Gaddafi to New York City and the New York Stock Exchange. Days later, war broke out in Libya and the "Khamis Brigade"—described in the media as led by Khamis Gaddafi—was involved in the attack on Benghazi, Libya.

When the media contacted AECOM, senior leaders approved Gennaro's strategy to be open and transparent about the nature of the internship and how the situation in Libya had changed dramatically since the internship began. Gennaro said there was a brief media frenzy over the internship but, because AECOM was fully transparent, the coverage was balanced and brief.

"For me, it was a great example of how quickly things move in the world; what is required of the CCO; and how we, if prepared and strategic, are uniquely positioned to help our organizations on numerous levels and at the most crucial junctures."

The role of steward of enterprise reputation is not strictly defensive. It also mandates seamless collaboration with enterprise brand-building efforts. This requires an understanding of the enterprise brand and leadership in shaping the approaches used to bring it to life, consistent with corporate character. This may involve strategic partnerships, new media, and other elements that mandate increased creativity and stakeholder engagement.

Kelly McGinnis, Levi Strauss & Co. CCO, believes that every interaction—and every employee—has an impact on an enterprise's reputation

(McGinnis 2016). McGinnis has helped change Levi's inwardly focused culture by unleashing the company's rich legacy and competitive spirit through storytelling that puts it at the center of cultural discussions. According to McGinnis:

> You can't build reputation if you're not authentic; and, for us, authenticity is all about trusted quality products, sincerity of action and heritage. Creative thinking around owned, earned, and paid media has enabled us to utilize platforms like LinkedIn and create new channels like our Unzipped hub to share our story, drive earned media and reshape perceptions about our company.

When it comes to reputation, McGinnis considers her role to "serve as the eyes and ears" of the company "to understand where the prevailing winds are headed and to drive how the company can influence those winds." In her 163-year-old enterprise, McGinnis says the CCO must "find new ways to tell our story, be inventive, and understand what's changing in the outside world while knowing the company through and through." By doing so, communication is "the bridge that helps take us from where we are to where we aspire to be."

Effective Communicator

Being able to execute business strategy requires effective, coordinated communication combined with keen strategic insight. The work of telling a brand's story, describing the rationale for enterprise actions and policies, and identifying the stakeholders with whom the enterprise must engage demands *competency as an effective communicator.*

With the proliferation of digital channels, and the more indirect influence that enterprises have in shaping perceptions, communicating honestly and effectively about the enterprise to key constituencies becomes even more crucial. Thus, the nature of the communication work that CCOs do—effectively and compellingly telling the truth—endures even as the tactics that are used—social, digital, content publishing—are transformed. This extends to enabling other leaders to effectively tell the company story.

As ExxonMobil CCO Suzanne McCarron (2016) notes, she and her public and government affairs team engage the public, policy makers, and stakeholders to increase understanding of the complex challenge of powering the world safely, efficiently, and responsibly. McCarron believes that energy literacy starts with telling the story of the role of energy in human progress. The most critical voice and leader in this effort is the chairman and CEO, who is supported, along with other senior leaders, through an executive communication operation that develops an integrated speech and media opportunity plan each year.

McCarron's team works with the business lines to review every invitation and opportunity to determine what the potential business value of the event is for ExxonMobil, and whether the event will strengthen relationships with key stakeholders. Once events are selected, they work with executives to craft speeches that draw on personal experiences, communicate ExxonMobil's optimistic vision for the future, and build understanding of the role of investment and innovation in shaping the modern energy landscape. ExxonMobil also works with its leaders to leverage other external communication channels. For example, it recently launched a new "content hub," EnergyFactor.com, which allows employees to share its story through social media.

Case: GE's Digital-Industrial Transformation and the Foundational Role of the CCO

The story of General Electric's (GE) transformation from a manufacturing company to the digital-industrial leader illustrates each aspect of the foundational CCO role. In 2012, when GE was making a fundamental strategy shift to infuse digital capabilities into all of its products and services, it turned to its communication team led by CCO Gary Sheffer to help it understand the business challenges and opportunities.[1]

---

[1] This case was written by chapter coauthor, Gary Sheffer. It is a recollection of his role in making a fundamental change in General Electric's business model through effective enterprise corporate communication.

The team responded with a stakeholder mapping and engagement strategy for CEO Jeff Immelt to network with and learn from leaders across digital industries. These experts, such as MIT's Andy McAfee, became advocates for GE's strategy to invest in its software and digital capabilities.

Sheffer, working with the company's economic research team, also analyzed public perceptions about the "industrial internet" on issues such as privacy, potential impact on jobs, and workplaces, and economic opportunities for businesses and individuals. As a result, GE issued several white papers to help establish strong thought leadership in a space that, to date, was not "owned" by any other company or enterprise.

Sheffer also used research to define the language GE would use in introducing itself to the tech world. As a 130-year-old industrial enterprise, GE was not known for its software expertise or identified as a Silicon Valley stalwart. Therefore, when Immelt introduced the strategy in the valley at a GE "Minds & Machines" event, he did so with a firm confidence in its success, while also acknowledging that GE had much to learn in the space. This sense of humility—and sense of humor—backed by highly visible actions and investments in the strategy, today pervades GE's thought leadership and brand-building as a "digital-industrial company."

GE's experience reflects the CCO's growing foundational role—helping a global enterprise understand the digital world and its leaders, enhancing its reputation in the space by grabbing "mind share" (which hopefully leads to market share), and then ensuring that strategy is communicated simply and persuasively to a broad set of stakeholders (including investors). "At GE, the expectations of the CCO are broader and more intense than ever," said Sheffer. "For CCOs, the foundational role now requires partnerships with everyone in the C-Suite and these leadership, reputation, and communication skills are more highly valued than ever."

Building the New Organization

In addition to the key elements of the foundational role, the CCO retains the enduring role of building the enterprise's communication function and attracting and retaining the best communication talent. Just as new skills are required of the CCO, they must also be developed, retained, and relearned across the entire Communication organization (see Chapter 9).

Case: GM's CCO on Transformational Change

A case in point can be found at General Motors, an enterprise in the midst of fundamental change as it leads a transformation in transportation that includes electrification and the emergence of autonomous vehicles. To support this shift, CCO Tony Cervone has redefined the work of the Communication organization. "We must become even stronger strategic business partners and even more proactive in using the right communication outlets to drive change and build reputation," says Cervone. "As the company becomes more customer-centered and attuned to the interests of key stakeholders, we must reflect this in our approach to communication as well" (Cervone 2016).

One key change relates to selecting what stories to tell (see Figure 6.1). "Historically, we tended to try to tell every GM story," Cervone says.

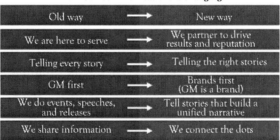

How GM communications is changing

Old way	→	New way
We are here to serve	→	We partner to drive results and reputation
Telling every story	→	Telling the right stories
GM first	→	Brands first (GM is a brand)
We do events, speeches, and releases	→	Tell stories that build a unified narrative
We share information	→	We connect the dots

Figure 6.1 GM communication change model

Now, we recognize the only way to tell the right stories is to be fully aligned with the business and its goals, to help us determine our strategy and narrative. We're trying to tell the right stories to the right media with the right audience.

As an example, the original PR plan for the Apple CarPlay and Android Auto announcement was to tell it as a General Motors story. This initial storyline highlighted that of the 35 vehicles offering Apple CarPlay in 2016, 30 would be GM vehicles. The media coverage generated would have been focused on GM. Instead, we identified a more customer-relevant strategy focused on "democratizing technology so our customers could use whatever phone they wanted ... across 14 models in the Chevrolet lineup." The results were twice that of our biggest estimated earned media reach of a technology story ever.

Cervone charged GM Communication executive Juli Huston-Rough and her team to research and define the skills, competencies, and behaviors required to support the new way of communication at GM. These competencies are essential to three key roles: modern communication expert, stakeholder engagement leader, and trusted partner (see Figure 6.2).

GM COMMUNICATION COMPETENCIES

	MODERN COMMUNICATION EXPERT	STAKEHOLDER ENGAGEMENT LEADER	TRUSTED PARTNER
SKILLS FOR COMMUNICATORS	Writing* Effective storytelling* Data analysis and insights* Understanding media Landscape* Visual assets News sense Crisis management Process Management/organizational skills	Media relations* Public speaking/company Spokesperson Effective storytelling* Employee Communication/engagement Authority and influence	Understands the business Strategic thinking candid Conversation/feedback Counseling Clients/business leaders Authority and influence
BEHAVIORS FOR COMMUNICATORS	Team focused Results oriented Always be curious Accountable	Act with a sense of purpose Act with integrity Diversity of thought Change agent	

*Indicates most important skills

Figure 6.2 GM communication competencies model

While skills like writing, storytelling, and media relations have always been important, GM is approaching them in new ways. According to Cervone,

Storytelling isn't simply a buzzword. Storytelling requires us to think holistically about the company's goals, the audiences we need to reach to achieve those goals, and additionally, use of the right words and visuals to communicate our perspective. We cannot be effective if we are telling stories in a vacuum.

Data and analytics are also taking on a particularly important role. "You have to use data to inform the success or failure of your efforts." "Communicators can no longer rely simply on their gut instincts alone, but instead, on their brains working together with their hearts," Cervone says.

In a digital-first world, it's easier than ever to get access to the data. The key is not to get lost in all the numbers but to ask the right questions of that data and watch it for trends or spikes that will lead to true insights.

As a result of our new approaches, the GM Communication team is a key, strategic business partner in driving major change at GM. Helping to lead this change is one of the most important things our Communication leadership team does.

Leading Diversity

Today's enterprise operates in an increasingly diverse marketplace with a multitude of stakeholder cultures, ideologies, experiences, interests, and actions. C-Suites, and even communication organizations, can never be fully representative of the composition of diverse stakeholder groups, although they must be more so than today. This underscores the need for a CCO who is cognizant of important distinctions and ensures the enterprise is responsive to them.

Achieving greater diversity and inclusion (D & I) is not only important because there is an ethical obligation to do so out of respect for distinct opinions and interests of stakeholders, but also because diversity of viewpoints makes an enterprise stronger and more competitive in the long run.

CCOs today have to be agents of change, particularly on diversity. Kimberly Goode, while serving as vice president of communication and corporate affairs at Northwestern Mutual, had access to a D & I team that was a central resource for the enterprise, in addition to a committee of senior executives who meet monthly to strategize and make decisions that drive diversity and inclusion within each functions.[2] All leaders in the company have a goal that they set based on where they are in their personal journey as a leader and department function head (Goode 2016).

For Goode this means driving change through her role at the corporate committee and through mentoring and coaching. She coaches colleagues to provide more experiences for employees as well as advocating for more people of color among the leadership ranks. She also supports a reverse mentoring program that matches senior executives with a nonsenior employee of a different race, gender, or background.

"This reverse mentoring experience helps our senior executives broaden their appreciation for difference and helps them grow in their diversity and inclusion journey," Goode said. "It pulls everyone out of their comfort zone and breaks barriers."

CCOs bear an important responsibility to facilitate an inclusive environment across the organization, says Ellen East, formerly of Time Warner Cable. But it is important for diversity to come from the top of the organization, and for Goode and her communication team, that level of C-Suite support make it possible to foster strong diversity and inclusion programs. "Leadership has to determine the company's core values, and for us, the importance of diversity and inclusion came right to the top," East said (2016). "But core values have to be more than a plaque on the wall; values have to show up in everyday behaviors, from the top down, and be reinforced in all of your communication." East noted that best practice is to incorporate diversity and inclusion goals in compensation, primarily as part of the bonus structure. When that incentive does not exist though, it is important for a CCO to challenge the enterprise and hold team members accountable for their actions.

Summary

The Foundational Role of the CCO

This foundational role as business leader, reputational steward, and effective communicator has long been central to the remit of the CCO.

---

[2] Goode is currently serving currently as senior vice president, external affairs at Blue Shield of California.

Indeed, it is the way the job is conventionally understood. Yet, in this changing business and communication landscape it has actually increased in scope, importance, and intensity. The changes described herein compound the need for a strong CCO who understands the enterprise and the forces affecting it, the diverse stakeholders impacted by the business and how to build relationships with them, and the dynamics of earning and maintaining the public's trust.

Most importantly, the CCO must be a vocal, compelling, and trusted counselor to the leadership, capable of guiding the enterprise on all of these fronts and articulating the consequences of failing to do so. Sound judgment, strong interpersonal skills, business and policy acumen, collaborative nature, diplomacy, cultural and social insight, and rhetorical prowess are only a few characteristics that are essential to the foundational role of the CCO. As Gary Sheffer, retired GE CCO, said in his introduction to the *The New CCO*, "It's a great time to be a CCO" (Arthur W. Page Society 2016, p. 3).

CHAPTER 7

Total Integration: Working Across the C-Suite

James S. O'Rourke, IV, James Spangler, and Richard Woods

The roles and responsibilities of today's chief communication officers (CCOs) are broader and more strategic than ever before, from creating communication strategies that drive business results, to managing key stakeholders within and outside of the organization, to developing and inspiring highly productive teams. Some CCOs have begun developing and overseeing digital engagement systems (DES, see Chapter 8 for more on this) designed to create enhanced stakeholder engagement. But where they really earn their paychecks and add the most value to an organization is in an interpersonal role: their ability to work effectively across the C-Suite. In fact, a strong case can be made that their primary responsibility *is* to work effectively across the C-Suite (see Harrison and Mühlberg 2014).

Why is this important? For any enterprise to achieve long-term success, it must be aligned at the top of the house. Its senior leadership teams must be united in understanding a *shared strategic direction and pursuing common business objectives*.[1] As noted in Chapter 4, such clarity and unity of purpose are essential to drive shareholder, stakeholder, and societal value. Everyone agrees that the CEO is the executive most responsible for creating and maintaining this alignment. But apart from her, the CCO is best positioned to make this happen.

---

[1] This is explained by Stacks (2017) and Michaelson and Stacks (2017) where they discuss "end-to-end" research, research focused on common problems affecting the enterprise's business goals and objectives.

This may sound unwarranted or overreaching. In practice, it is anything but. Quite frankly, other C-Suite executives have all-consuming responsibilities within their specific functional areas. They are focused on managing business or functional excellence—aligned with the corporate strategies—downward within their respective areas of responsibility. Apart from the CEO, the CCO is the only other senior generalist in the C-Suite (c.f., Harrison and Mühlberg 2014). Of the senior management team, only the CCO shares responsibility with the CEO for ensuring that key corporate strategies and initiatives are *understood and acted upon* enterprisewide. The CCO does this by working *across* the C-Suite: advising, supporting, and ensuring that the enterprise mission, vision, and values are being supported by the other leaders in driving this understanding and alignment.

Additionally, the CCO shares with the CEO responsibility for instilling across the enterprise the "corporate character," as discussed in Chapter 4 and described in the Page Model and reports that further examined its application within the enterprise (2012a, 2013b, 2014, 2016.), including its values, mission, vision, purpose, and culture. As we have seen in many post hoc analyses of crisis communication, employees who understand and exemplify corporate character reduce negative crisis outcomes, specifically in terms of reputation and costs (Coombs 2017). Customers must perceive and believe in it. Marketing's (CMO) efforts to build the brand and drive sales should reflect it. Operations (COO) and Finance (CFO) must execute in a way that is consistent with it. Human Resources (CHRO) ought to reflect it, as well, in the way it fosters a positive enterprise corporate culture, supportive of all stakeholders (see Chapter 6). The CCO, then, is charged with *operationalizing* corporate character throughout the enterprise so it becomes the foundation of organizational identity and image, and is evident in all its actions.

For the CCO, working across the C-Suite has two facets. The first is understanding and championing the CEO's vision and desired culture enterprisewide. The second is serving as a value-added collaborator with fellow C-Suite executives, connecting their accomplishments and their victories in each functional area to the prospective success of the entire business. This *collaborative* role is the principal reason why many senior communication leaders regard themselves and their teams as "connectors" within their enterprises. The benefits of this role are also twofold. First, by working closely with fellow members of the C-Suite, CCOs can both help these executives to be more effective in driving understanding and alignment within their respective functional areas. Second, they enhance their own grasp of what is happening enterprisewide. These added insights can be invaluable to a CCO's role as the integrator at the top of the house, using the ability to counsel message strategies from an enterprise 360° perspective throughout the C-Suite.

The New CCO and the Importance of Integration

The Arthur Page Society's groundbreaking 2016 report, *The New CCO: Transforming Enterprises in a Changing World*, identified this "integrator" responsibility as critical, even central to the CCO's role.

> One of our hypotheses was that we would see new organizational structures emerging, with particular focus on the relative positions of Communication and Marketing. We instead discovered a more important emerging recognition that formal structure and ownership matter less than the CCO's ability to drive cross-functional collaboration and integration around strategic priorities. Indeed, as noted earlier, engagement by the CCO with other C-Suite members is growing in regularity and importance. (p. 25)

Much debate has arisen about the convergence of various functions—primarily communication and marketing—and who owns what, where there is inherent overlap. Does the CMO own the brand, or does the CHRO own the culture or recruitment/retention, when these are inextricably tied to enterprise corporate character? Does the chief information officer (CIO) own digital platforms when these must be built around a customer or employee need? Does the General Counsel own risk mitigation when stakeholder relationships are a vital element of issues management?

In today's enterprise, the question of "who owns what" is far less important than an ability for the "what" to be closely coordinated across functions. This is the CCO's consummate contribution, serving as the enterprise strategist, creating messaging, and integrating these into organizational action campaigns that make disparate functions operate as a unified whole.

The New CCO offers the observations of Leah Johnson, CEO of LCJ Solutions, who summed it up nicely:

> In my experience, those CCOs who have very strategic roles within an organization naturally act as the integration chief. They have the ability to look out across the entire organization, within businesses and across other functions, to understand goals and integrate messaging and activities. Reporting structure rarely matters here. What matters is getting parties to the table to work well together and see the value of integration. (p. 25)

Case: Capital One's Integrated Approach to Managing Enterprise Risk

A product development team needed to get buy-in for a new product from a reputation risk standpoint and arranged for a meeting with Capital One's CCO (whose function is labeled "Corporate Affairs") a day before they were scheduled to present it to the CEO. The team had invested months calibrating every aspect of the product and was expecting ready approval.[2]

However, as the presentation unfolded, it became apparent that, for all its virtues, the product would fail to meet the stakeholder expectations of at least one key community and consumer advocacy group. The problem was simple: it would create an unacceptable level of reputation risk for the company.

Hearing this, the product team responded by observing that it would be "too expensive," "too complex," and "unrealistic" to remedy the problem to the satisfaction of these groups and, to support their position, they offered extensive consumer research, financial models, and operational expertise. The case for reputation risk, on the other hand, drew upon "soft" data, such as the judgment of stakeholder

---

[2] *Source*: Richard Woods, SVP of Corporate Affairs, Capital One Financial.

group experts who acknowledged that they were asking the product team to pay a known and measurable price today as insurance against a reputation setback that would be difficult to value and which might, in fact, never happen.

Corporate Affairs was challenged to deliver value up through a three-level hierarchy that began at the first, most basic level by helping the company "say it," followed by crafting "what to say" and, finally, by helping the company decide "what to do." Achieving the top of this hierarchy is too often haphazard and opportunistic. If a Corporate Affairs function is to realize its full potential as strategic partner to the business lines or to succeed in managing the enterprise's reputation to a meaningful degree, the CCO requires a firm commitment from leadership and a formal process to support it.

Capital One embraced the strategic importance of this by implementing a management discipline that sees reputational risk as an integral part of business decision making, much the same as credit risk or operating risk. This management process was designed to:

- Address decisions made enterprisewide;
- Systematically engage product managers, line of business heads, members of the executive committee (C-Suite) and the board;
- Adhere to auditable processes consistent with the bank's other risk management programs; and
- Produce measurable outcomes.

Today, Capital One's formal Reputation Risk Management Program has three foundational components:

1. *Enterprise Reputation Risk Policy:* Holds the enterprise responsible to its Board of Directors for managing its affairs within a defined "risk appetite."
2. *Enterprise Reputation Risk Standard:* Defines specific executive accountabilities and the processes to which the company must adhere in implementing the Policy, including the frequency

and form of reporting to the company's internal and Board risk committees. The Standard names a member of the Executive Committee as the "enterprise reputation risk steward" and the CCO is the "designated reputation risk executive."

3. *Business Line Procedures:* Outlines the requirements that the business lines must apply in order to implement the enterprise level standards.

Recognizing early on that, to be successful, reputation management would require input from experts in stakeholder relations who were organized in functions outside of Corporate Affairs, Capital One formed a cross-functional team called the Reputation Risk Council composed of these experts and their peers in Corporate Affairs.

The Council is chaired by the CCO and is the body responsible for making assessments of enterprise-level reputation risk. Council members bring to this task decades of experience with their individual stakeholder groups, as well as insights gleaned from opinion research, statistical trends in customer satisfaction and complaints, employee engagement scores, and corporate reputation rankings.

To drive reputation risk considerations deep into the enterprise business lines, Corporate Affairs also designates a member of its team to be the reputation risk advisor to each business line, so that they can take reputation risk into account at the earliest stages of product development.

The CCO submits a quarterly "enterprise reputation risk report" to members of the internal and Board-level risk committees that marks trends in stakeholder group attitudes, details risks arising from each business line, and summarizes the enterprise's overall reputation risk exposure. The report in its entirety reflects the integrated view of the Council.

Occasionally, a proposed decision has the potential to create a level of reputational risk that exceeds enterprise risk appetite. In such cases, the Standard describes an "escalation path" and formal communication sequence that begins with the product manager, moves to the business line head, and *could* include the members of the Executive Committee, the CEO, and the Board, depending on circumstances.

> Over the past 10 years, Capital One's Reputation Risk Management Program has made consideration of reputational risk a routine part of business decision making. It has also systematized engagement from Capital One stakeholder experts, including members of the enterprise corporate communication team, at every level of the value hierarchy.

Analysis

Arthur W. Page observed that "all business in a democratic country begins with public permission and exists by public approval."[3] Capital One's Reputation Risk Management Program has been designed to apply this observation to the conduct of its business.

Communicating with the "Audience of One"

How should a CCO approach the role of integrator? It may sound paradoxical, but we recommend starting out with an "audience of one," with that primary audience being the CEO.

More than anyone or anything else, it is the CEO who sets the vision and shapes the culture of the enterprise through her words and actions. The CCO's "integrator" role begins with a deep understanding of corporate vision, values, and culture and helping the CEO implement them enterprise wide.

The "audience of one" concept was introduced to one of this chapter's authors, Jim Spangler on June 9, 2016, as he was leaving the professional services firm Andersen Worldwide to join Tenneco Automotive, a global supplier of automotive components, as the head of communication in late 1999. The idea came from John Newton, a seasoned, UK-based communication consultant who had served Andersen Worldwide for more than 20 years, including many years spent working with Jim Wadia, the

---

[3] Page, Arthur W., in a speech on "Industrial Statesmanship" to a Public Relations Conference sponsored by the Chesapeake & Ohio Railway Company, White Sulpher Springs, VA, October 27, 1939. Full text available online from The Arthur W. Page Center, Bellisario College of Communication, Pennsylvania State University. http://comm.psu.edu/page-center/speech/industrial-statesmanship

firm's CEO. Newton mentored Spangler in his working relationship with Wadia when Spangler headed up the firm's global media relations and public relations functions. As Spangler recalled:

> I asked John how he had earned Wadia's trust. He told me he worked relentlessly to stay on top of the business priorities and problems that were most important to Wadia at a particular time, and to recommend communications strategies to help Wadia achieve his business goals.

> Then John looked me square in the eye, and in all seriousness told me that in order to be successful at Tenneco, I had one priority—"focus on the CEO. Work with him to drive his vision for the company and his business objectives."

> Viewed with a different emphasis, one of the CCO's top priorities is to help the CEO win.

Securing the Credibility Required to Be Influential

While the need for "audience of one" focus is imperative, reaching a career point where the CCO has the ability to make such an impact can itself be daunting. To be effectively positioned to do this, CCOs must do more than command a proven skill set. To win a seat at the table (Grunig 1984), they must also build influence through *credibility*. And to do this, they must successfully navigate the challenging C-Suite environment, articulate a clear and distinct perspective, and demonstrate value through action. With credibility comes C-Suite leadership (c.f., Harrison and Mühlberg 2014).

Let's face it: CEOs are an extremely competitive lot, and many of them have healthy egos to match. They hate to lose, and most are at their best solving complex, rapidly changing business issues. Only the toughest issues rise to their level. And their decisions affect hundreds if not thousands of stakeholders, starting with their own employees; they also often include those working for their suppliers and customers. CEO choices also affect investors at all levels, from money managers overseeing funds worth billions to the small retirement savings of an ageing retired school nurse. Their conclusions and actions also have worldwide consequences.

CEOs, in other words, are accustomed to making tough calls. The good ones surround themselves with smart people with driving ambitions, hard-won experiences, and deeply ingrained points of view. To make a difference in helping the CEO win, a CCO must first become a true management team member, and then have a relationship based on courage and conviction to convince a CEO, who is accustomed to being the smartest in the room, to consider their counsel and follow their advice. To do this requires both articulating a distinct perspective and demonstrating value with action. One must be able to help the CEO achieve her goals when she's right, and to have the courage and ability to tell her what she needs to hear when she's wrong.

Securing Credibility

To secure credibility, CCOs and their teams must develop communication plans that feature a bias for *action*. Further, those plans must have goals consistent with the enterprise and focus on measureable objectives correlated to other functions, as well as enterprise success (Stacks 2017). Consider the CEO's perspective; her fate with the Board of Directors depends on the successful articulation of enterprise strategy and effective pursuit of business objectives, resulting in the best achievable performance results. The CCO begins earning the trust of the CEO by creating enterprise strategies that focus on mission, vision, values, and cultural variables that assist the chief executive in a clearly and concisely communicating that strategy and business goals to key stakeholders, inside and outside the company. But to deliver maximum benefit to the CEO, the result must be more than awareness or alignment. *The ultimate objective, in fact, must be stakeholder buy-in and action.*

Strategic Outlook

A great place to start is internally. For example, while heading up Communication at Tenneco, Inc., Spangler and his team worked with the CEO to develop a single PowerPoint slide that concisely defined what *winning* looked like in a particular year for the enterprise and its 19,000 employees worldwide (see Figure 7.1). The slide contained four business metrics that every employee could understand, from plant operators to

Figure 7.1 Strategic winning at Tenneco

senior leadership team members. Each functional group and business unit then took those four metrics and developed its own one-page slide, which clearly articulated its "piece" of the overall corporate goals. From an *alignment* perspective, this approach proved valuable: line workers at nearly any Tenneco plant in the world could tell a visiting executive how their work contributed to plant and enterprise goals, but the ultimate benefit was improved corporate *performance*.[4]

Reflecting this bias toward action, the CCO—like all functional leaders—must meet regularly with the CEO to stay abreast of her top business priorities, goals, and issues, while updating her on how the Communication team is implementing and evaluating key communication programs designed to drive awareness, alignment, buy-in, and action around those key business objectives. It helps if all stakeholder engagement strategies—internal and external—are linked to specific CCO key performance indicators (KPI) measures,[5] so the CCO can show, in business terms, how her actions and those of the functional team are supporting the business. Further, by incorporating these metrics into the enterprise's own evaluation system (e.g., Six Sigma, Balanced Scorecard) and correlating them to

---

[4] Actual finances and percent benchmark objectives have been redacted as proprietary data of Tenneco.

[5] For definitions of key research and strategy terms, please see the *Dictionary of Public Relations Research and Measurement* (3rd ed.) by Stacks and Bowen (2013). The *Dictionary* is available at no cost from the Institute for Public Relations (www.instituteforpr.org) in six different languages.

other functional outcomes, communication outcomes can be correlated to specific functional outcomes and business objectives. A company with an absenteeism problem, for example, might target a communication campaign on the importance of being on the job, and then track absenteeism rates with other company KPIs—such as product quality, pride in ownership, sales, GAP data—and correlate communication outcomes (such as decreased absenteeism) with other functional outcomes over time. These metrics also help the CCO run the function, identifying areas where performance is on track meeting both informational and motivational objectives, or exceeding expectations, while pointing out any gaps requiring corrective action.

Once the CCO understands the CEO's objectives, and has developed communication plans to support them, she can then work to drive this alignment across the enterprise, starting at the top with the senior leadership team in the C-Suite.

Building Effective Relationships Across the C-Suite

If knowledge is power, as the adage goes, then influence is power's first cousin. In achieving CCO impact across the C-Suite, influence is the name of the game, according to Bruce Harrison (2016), a longtime Page Society member who until recently taught crisis communication and leadership to graduate students at Georgetown University. "Without it [influence], the effort is just not likely to be effective. It starts with understanding the business—those are table stakes in the C-Suite," says Harrison.

As spelled out in *The New CCO* (2016, p. 21), the foundational role of today's CCO includes the roles of "business strategist, guardian of reputation and builder of stakeholder relationships" (see Chapter 6). Given the highly strategic aspect of this role, today's CCO must become knowledgeable in all aspects of the business. This is best accomplished by building collaborative working relationships with fellow senior leaders.

Strategic Outlook

The process for building such relationships is simple and mirrors the approach taken with the CEO, starting with spending time with them, asking questions, and listening carefully to the answers.

Regardless of experience as a CCO, the best advice is to begin with leaders who have profit and loss (P&L) responsibility, including the COO (if there is one) and business group or division leaders. Initial outreach should also focus on individuals in roles with whom the CCO has built-in collaboration requirements, based on shared responsibilities for engagement with key stakeholders. These generally include the CHRO, CMO, CFO, and frequently the chief of investor relations (CIRO), as well as the head of government relations, if not in the CCO portfolio.

Working with both categories of leader, today's CCO must put herself in her colleagues' position and mindset, and understand what they are dealing with, in order to offer sound counsel regarding effective communication and stakeholder engagement strategies, expressed in terms they can understand.

At this point, the "audience of one" that focused on the CEO should pivot to an "audience of one at a time." Although this is common sense for the seasoned CCO, meeting each functional leader is not always the first thing on the inexperienced CCO's mind. Before such meetings, learn as much as possible about each executive's background and businesses or functions. Create a list of "smart" questions. Being buttoned down and prepared like this will greatly enhance your brand.

Make the meeting "all about them" to find out what is important to them and how they run their businesses. Ask them to brief on their key priorities, short and long term. Seek to understand how their objectives contribute to the overall enterprise goals. Identify their two to three *key business issues*, including the number-one problem facing them at that moment. Who are their customers? Competitors? Key suppliers? Where are their operations located? Which geographical markets are hot; which are not? Among the Page Principles is "Listen to the stakeholder"; other functional leaders are primary stakeholders who can offer a clearer understanding of enterprise strategies. Listen and learn. In addition to getting an invaluable primer on their operations, this meeting provides insights into how each executive is wired—from the way they manage their teams to how they prioritize their time.

Before wrapping up, spend some time getting their thoughts on how the communication function is currently supporting them. Ask them what is working, and what you or your team could do better. Try to get them to be as specific as possible; questions might include asking their opinions on the CEO's communication strengths and weaknesses (create a Strengths, Weaknesses, Opportunities, Threats (SWOT) analysis), and where or how the CEO can be more effective in driving alignment and action around the enterprise's vision and business goals.

This last part is important, because it provides insight into how each of these executives views communication. Be prepared; their answers will vary greatly. But, again, the insights will help develop deeper individual relationships.

Thank each one for their time and promise to follow up with them in 30 days or so. In fact, try to schedule a follow-up meeting at that time.

This type of contact sends several messages to those you meet with:

1. *The CCO is a team player*, a serious business executive focused on enterprise priorities and business.
2. *The CCO understands the enterprise objectives*, and is serious about creating measureable communication strategies designed to help achieve enterprise goals. And;
3. *The CCO can offer strategies to effectively communicate with stakeholders* that will help achieve functional goals.

Exchange your findings with your subfunction lieutenants, and begin brainstorming how this intelligence affects team communication objectives, goal, and programs. This will generate new ways to drive better business performance through strategic communication plans and programs aimed at problem solving across the enterprise.

Follow-up meetings will be essential; next time, make those meetings all about the communication function. Come back to each executive and share communication plans (at a high level) for the enterprise, as well as ideas for helping them achieve their goals. Then, ask for their input. Their responses will provide a good gauge not only on their buy-in to the plan, but on their attitudes toward the role communication can play in helping them succeed. Again, these attitudes will vary greatly from executive to executive, but at least you will know where your function stands.

With functional leaders, look for opportunities to collaborate on key initiatives. The annual investor day is one such opportunity. Other than the four quarterly reports, investor day is the single most important day in the Chief Investor Relations Officer's annual calendar. It is important that the CIRO and CCO work together to put the enterprise's best foot forward with investors, insuring that enterprise mission, vision, values—and often culture—are clearly reflected in the messages aimed at financial stakeholders. Offer your team to review scripts. Take part in developing overall themes (again, focusing on mission, vision, values, and cultural variables). Offer the function's writers to work on key executives' scripts and slides; be personally involved in the CEO's script. Keep in mind, your CEO expects her CCO to be intimately involved, even if not expressly charged with doing so. CEOs do not care about lines of responsibility, such as the CIRO being responsible for a successful investor day. They just want results and expect key leaders to work together for the benefit of the company.

The next step in cross-functional integration is as important as the first two: *execute the communication plan and provide measureable results that have been correlated with other functional objectives driving the business plan.* Up to this point, the CCO has merely established a foundation for building trust. Execution is where CCOs and their teams start to make deposits in building trust and value within the C-Suite.

Case: CCO Jim Spangler's Integration Across Navistar's Enterprise

When Jim Spangler joined Navistar as its CCO in June of 2011, he recognized that investor relations, government relations, marketing, and communication were operating in a narrow "silo mentality."[6] This was confirmed in his first sit-down meeting with Jack Allen, who headed up Navistar's largest business unit, the North America

---

[6] This case examines how Jim Spangler integrated his role as a new CCO in an enterprise through a strategic approach to his entry into Navistar's C-Suite. Navistar is a Fortune 500 company and a leading manufacturer of commercial trucks, buses, defense vehicles, and engines (www.navistar.com).

Truck and Bus group. Allen felt the company needed to do a better job speaking with "one voice" externally, and recommended that Spangler solve this problem.

He immediately set out to establish collaborative working relationships with his peers who were heading up IR, government relations, and marketing. Additionally, he set up a joint communication council with the functions, which met regularly to plan and discuss consistent messaging, as well as to plan major programs within and outside particular functional responsibilities.

The value of the "one voice" process was evident early in his assignment at Navistar, when it launched a major turnaround and installed an interim CEO. The process proved valuable for effectively announcing the changes to internal and external stakeholders; and in the subsequent months, it helped position the company in the best possible light as it worked through its turnaround.

Based on previous experience, Spangler knew that some executives would take him seriously, but others would be harder to win over, if ever. Some would believe in the power and importance of communication, while others were likely to be skeptics. By engaging with those who were willing to engage with him, and being relentlessly persistent with those who were not, he was able to integrate him and his functional team into the C-Suite as an influential and vital partner with an understanding of the business and the responsibilities of other C-Suite functional leaders. These strategies maintain a long-game perspective where communication strategy is built into each function's plans, as well as the overall enterprise business plan.

The key to success was to build his personal brand and his team's brand as people who get results while helping others get results. Building trusting relationships opens the door to enhanced influence across the C-Suite. By working closely with C-Suite peers, Spangler became more knowledgeable and up-to-date on the business of Navistar and better positioned the communications function to add value to the enterprise.

Summary

The CCO is uniquely positioned to help drive enterprise corporate leadership in achieving their goals and objectives. Through *measureable* communication programs that reflect the enterprise's mission, vision, values, and culture the CCO helps to develop corporate culture and build internal and external stakeholder beliefs. This includes both helping the CEO articulate her goals and strategies, and helping other members of the C-Suite drive these goals and strategies both inside and outside the organization. As such, the CCO is the executive best positioned to be the "integrator" across the C-Suite, making sure the leadership team is working together to execute the CEO's vision.

To achieve this, influence is the name of the game. To be influential, an enterprise officer requires credibility and trust, which can be gained only by building relationships and demonstrating commitment and understanding—first with the CEO, then with other members of the C-Suite.

Building such relationships works in two ways. First, you help them to be more effective with their teams. And second, in return, they will help you to be more effective with your CEO. It is a virtuous circle. Relationships and commitment help to build trust. In turn, trust builds influence.

This involves the same skill sets CCOs develop as they build their careers: listening, engaging, and persuading. CCOs must listen effectively to others' concerns and perspectives; they must examine their colleagues' positions and mindsets, seeking to understand what they are dealing with; then, they must offer sound counsel in terms they can understand.

Often this takes courage. The CCO must tell others what they *need* to hear, all the while being polite, persistent, and professional. The ultimate measure of a communicator's success will be her embodiment of the Page Principles and her performance as a postmodern communication professional (Arthur W. Page Society 2016, pp. 28, 38).

CHAPTER 8

Building an Enterprise Digital Engagement System

Terence (Terry) Flynn, Jon Iwata, and Alan Marks

Historically, businesses have engaged their stakeholders primarily through intermediaries—through mass media (both earned and owned content) to broadly disseminate an enterprise's purpose and point of view and build stakeholder support, complementing and reinforcing direct interaction with stakeholders (see Chapter 5, note 1). The enterprise's communication function was largely in control of the earned-media dimensions of this engagement, managing it through discrete channels and utilizing *push messaging* to broad audience segments.[1]

Today, technology has upended these engagement models. Consider:

- More than 5 billion people use mobile phones, about three-quarters of the world's population (Constine and Escher May 27, 2015).
- 65 percent of adults in the United States now use social networking sites—a nearly 10-fold increase from 2005 to 2015. Women and men are using social media at nearly the same rates. One-fifth of Americans say they are online "almost constantly." Three out of four go online daily (Perrin October 8, 2015).
- There are 3.5 billion Google searches every day (Internet Live Stats n.d.).

---

[1] Push messaging is one-way, asymmetric communication with inside–outside message flow.

- 90 percent of smartphone users share their location data by using location services (Pew Research Center January 20, 2016).
- 104.3 million wearables were shipped in 2016, a number expected to double in just five years (IDC June 21, 2017).
- There are 94.3 million subscribers to Netflix streaming services (ReCode April 17, 2017).
- The average consumer belongs to 13 loyalty programs (Ad Age June 17, 2015).
- There were 12.4 million connected cars in 2016, going to 61,000,000 in 2020 (Gartner September 29, 2016).

People are sharing data about themselves at every moment—what they like, think, and eat; where they are and where they are going; their nutrition and fitness; their media, entertainment, and political preferences. All of these data are captured digitally, and people expect companies and institutions to provide value to them based on that data. The organizations that provide a more personalized experience, a better recommendation, time savings, and inspiration are the organizations that win mindshare and lasting affiliation.

At the same time, an organization's stakeholders are no longer solely "consumers" or "audiences." They are content *creators* in their own right. The same technologies enable them not just to receive but to transmit. On social media every minute there are:

- 30,000 minutes of YouTube video uploaded;
- 3.3 million Facebook posts;
- 448,800 tweets;
- 65,900 Instagram photos uploaded;
- 1,440 blogs posted on Wordpress;
- 29 million messages sent on WhatsApp (Smart Insights February 6, 2017).

Like, share, comment: The ability for anyone to perform these simple actions about virtually anything, to virtually everyone, is redefining how enterprises now pursue stakeholder engagement. In less than a decade, social media tools and platforms have evolved from novelty to ubiquity. These are the most personalized media ever experienced (c.f., Li and Stacks 2015), and they generate influence and engagement at a pace and scale unimaginable just a few years ago. Mobile technology has significantly accelerated this new reality. Combined with the predictive power of "big data" analytics,[2] digital engagement is transforming how we live, work, and interact with each other.

In this new world, transparency and authenticity are at a premium. "Mass" is out; "personal" is in. "Freedom of the press" used to mean "freedom for those who own one." Today, everyone with a smartphone is a media mogul, free to speak his or her mind, start a campaign—and engage an enterprise.

Employees can freely share news and opinions about their company with their friends, family members, career contacts, and future potential employees. Investors can activate other investors. Customers can write product reviews that are viewed by prospective customers on the other side of the world. Conversations between vendors and customers are transparent.

All of this content is highly influential. Eighty-two percent of U.S. adults use online reviews before making a first-time purchase (Pew Research Center December 19, 2016); 61 percent of job seekers look at company reviews and ratings before making a decision to apply for a job (Glassdoor 2016); and 60 percent of people rate "a person like myself" as credible as an academic or technical expert (2017 Edelman Trust Barometer January 5, 2017).

This is not new news to CCOs. The opportunity for communicators to engage more people directly or through other people they trust, with

---

[2] "Big data" has been defined as extremely large, nonstructured data sets where the variables can create new variables based on the data being gathered. Big data is typically culled from ongoing Internet connectivity and requires high processing speed and data storage bases. "Large data" can be as huge as big data, but the data are structured in such a way that any new variables must be created by the data analyst or researcher; it is usually used to examine stakeholder norms. "Small data" is typically a reduced variable, structured data set; it is typically used to test hypotheses or answer research questions (Stacks 2017).

exponentially more personal impact, has been known and explored at the edges for years. But fully realizing the opportunity can only be achieved by changing the profession's old model. This is not just about better use of social media. For one, it would be impossible to hire enough communications professionals to engage directly at the scale now required. These technology-driven social and cultural trends are changing the role of the CCO. In addition to relationships and reporters, CCOs must be able deploy intelligent algorithms and automation.

To create personalized, predictive engagement of individuals, CCOs and the functions they lead require new skills, a new mindset, and new digital capability. Together, these make up a comprehensive Digital Engagement System (DES).

What Is a Digital Engagement System?

As defined in *The New CCO* (2016), published by the Page Society, a DES harnesses "sophisticated platforms that map stakeholders, engender understanding of them (usually through data) and systematize the process of engaging with them, not merely as segments but as individuals" (p. 32).

Other enterprise functions have long established analogous systems and processes that permeate the organization. Human resources runs systems that address people management and the talent resources of the enterprise. Marketing has them to manage the customer's journey through the marketing funnel. Legal has them to ensure compliance and mitigate enterprise risk. The CCO must similarly become the architect and manager of systems that *engage* enterprise stakeholders, internally and externally, with content and information that builds trust, fosters commitment, and facilitates action (see Chapter 7).

To understand what we mean by a "Digital Engagement System," we must look at each word—because each word matters.

It is *Digital* because digital is where our stakeholders' data are captured, and because digital is the only way to engage them individually at scale.

It is about *Engagement* because organizational communications can no longer be based on a "messaging" model. We must create dialogue, and dialogue requires not just speaking, but listening—and intelligent, appropriate, *personalized* responses.

And it is a *System* because it is structured into something greater than the sum of its parts. It senses and responds to feedback. It can be measured and managed, and it can operate continuously.

The essential connected elements in this system are:

- The data that fuel it;
- The content that shapes the organization's dialogue with its stakeholders;
- Its underlying technologies;
- The professionals with the skills and discipline to operate the system, measure success, and improve based on feedback.

Data

Every DES both runs on and generates data—data about who your stakeholders are, what they are saying, what they are doing, what they like, and how they consume, create, and share content. There are also data about trending topics in the world, financial market performance, hyperlocal weather forecasts with their connection to commerce and mood, and data on the effectiveness of specific content.

Some of these data likely already exist in your company. Partners like the Chief Information Officer (CIO) or Chief Human Resources Officer (CHRO) will be critical in helping you obtain data such as employee information (role, tenure), web or intranet data (what customers and employees visit, download, and share; time spent; traffic flow), e-mail data (click-through rates, open rates, downloads, forwards), and more. Other data can be licensed, retrieved from public sources, or mined using artificial intelligence. And some data must be created through designed experiments.

Content

In a DES, "content" refers to intellectual capital deliberately created by participants in the organization's ecosystem, inside and outside the company. This content comes in many forms—videos, podcasts, social tiles, articles, infographics, white papers, and beyond. It shapes a dialogue of content exchange—an exchange that is strategically stimulated and managed.

Data are key to that purposeful management. For instance, topics for new content are discovered through mining data. Multiple versions of a piece are tried, tested, and updated based on performance data. Pride of authorship is less important than what works best.

And whatever the form or purpose, the content must be designed to be shared. It must not only be compelling and provocative, but also configured appropriately for various social platforms so it is easy to use and says something about the person sharing it.

Technology

DESs require a range of technologies. These technologies are available for every scale and purpose, often with free or freemium models, as well as premium versions. They may already be at work in another part of your business, such as under the CMO. Examples include:

- Content and Workflow Management technologies to help your professionals create, edit, manage, and deploy content as appropriate to your customers or employees. Today, tools like this include Drupal and Alfresco.
- Data Management and Insights technologies to help you spot trends and patterns in social media conversations that may trigger targeted engagement, distribution of content already in the content management system, or new ideas for content that should be created. Today, Zignal and Marketo make tools for this purpose.
- Distribution technologies to help you find the right audience for your content, promote it, and deliver it to many individuals, at scale. Tools available today include Hootsuite and Sprinklr.

People

DESs require professionals with specific skills. They fall into four primary categories:

- **Listening**—Communication professionals must be able to find the channels where their audiences engage and listen to the themes and data they are generating, identifying trends and patterns as they emerge as well as finding influencers across ecosystems. Listening is the first step to building effective engagement with the constituents that matter to your organization.

- **Editorial and creative**—Communication professionals must create content designed to engage individuals at scale, based on listening and overall communications strategy. These skills probably exist on your teams today but may need to evolve to support new media.

- **Engagement**—Beyond mere publication, communication professionals must share content and participate in dialogue with individuals, including sharing content those individuals have created. They might seed initial engagement through the use of paid media and then amplify the contributions of people who are participating in the conversation with more paid media. They are constantly acting on trends in conversation and responding to direct questions or comments.

- **Technologists**—To support the earlier work, you need professionals who deeply understand the DES and can implement and customize the tools that underpin it. The more integrated these professionals are with the listening, editorial, and creative professionals, the more quickly the DES can adapt to achieve better outcomes.

Some cutting-edge CCOs have already started to create new roles and to train their teams on the new skills required for this model—roles that previously did not exist, like content and engagement designer, web DJ, digital strategist, behavioral scientist, and culture czar ("The New CCO," p. 17). Seventy-three percent of respondents to a Page Society poll of CCOs conducted as part of the New CCO report said that they are hiring digital or social media experts. They are also shifting their resources toward content creation. Thirty percent of CCOs who participated in the Page Jam—a two-day online discussion among senior communicators convened by Page—indicated they are rapidly increasing investment in owned media. In addition, 25 percent are hiring big data analysts (Weber Shandwick 2014).

Big Data and the Digital PlayBook

Leveraging data is an essential component of an effective DES. Increasingly this means harnessing "big data," in addition to the more conventional large and small data sets used in normal business processes and measurement dashboards. This is made possible by the unprecedented amount of data generated by the technology we use every day, combined with affordable computing and storage. In virtually every field, businesses, governments, enterprises, and researchers are learning how to leverage enormous amounts of data to create predictive models that lead to new insights and new ways of creating and delivering value.

For CCOs, leveraging big data in ways that are relevant to enterprise goals and objectives represents an extraordinary opportunity to create economic value and competitive advantage, build more integrative, collaborative C-Suite strategies, and drive enterprise-wide approaches to reputation management, influence, and advocacy.

Big data are being applied in almost every area of business. Human Resources, for example, is active in its use of big data analytics. Predictive models are being used to assess hiring and identify the best candidates, manage attrition, and flag other potential outcomes that help an enterprise manage a high-performing culture and workforce. For the CCO, this trend creates opportunity to partner with the CHRO and use big data insights to sharpen and better target employee engagement strategies and content. Such predictive models also can be used to inform employee brand and externally focused reputation management strategies.

CHRO Partnering

Predictive models based on employee data and external market and competitive data reveal trigger points that can be influenced by targeted content and personalized engagement. A predictive model, for example, shows that a certain segment of employees in a technology enterprise are vulnerable to leaving at a certain time of year, or with a certain frequency. Armed with that insight, a communication team creates targeted content to the employees' manager, reminding the manager to personally engage the team, conduct one-to-one check-in discussions, and ensure the team understands the importance of their work to the entire enterprise. At the same time, personalized content is sent to each employee on the team, highlighting his or her role and contributions to the enterprise's overall strategy. Other targeted content may highlight enterprise culture, benefits, and values, reminding these employees how competitive and desirable the enterprise is as a place to work. Complementing this targeted content, stories profiling the team's work and successes are sent across the enterprise, reinforcing the targeted messages and manager engagement. At scale, the DES automates these activities across multiple internal stakeholder constituencies—employees, managers, and leaders throughout the entire enterprise. The results: lower attrition, higher engagement, and more effective people management.

Partnering with the CMO to effectively harness customer data is an obvious area of engagement. Sales and customer service functions are other areas that generate enormous amounts of data that can yield competitive insights and predictive models. And there are many sources of third-party data that, when combined with enterprise-proprietary data, unleash fresh insights and opportunities.

CMO Partnering

1. A DES automatically distributes customized market, sales, product, and competitive content to the mobile phones of the enterprise's sales executives, based on their geolocation data, as well as proprietary customer and other third-party market data. Regardless of where sales executives travel, they know they will have up-to-date customer, market, and competitive content on their mobile phone, enabling them more effectively to drive customer engagement, deliver customer value, and win new business.

2. An irate customer writes about a negative experience on social media. Other customers have had similar experiences and share their stories (perhaps including smartphone videos), and the issue quickly gains traction. Another customer launches an online petition to force the enterprise to respond. Within hours, calls begin to spike in the enterprise's customer call center and the enterprise begins receiving media inquiries about the issue. Leveraging a DES, the communication team quickly analyzes available enterprise data regarding the issue, assesses customer call patterns, maps the social media influence of the customers participating in the discussion, and identifies relevant media interested in the issue. The DES enables the communication team quickly to develop and deliver targeted content: talking points to customer service representatives, direct messages to aggrieved customers and targeted media relations outreach to relevant media. In addition, the enterprise quickly develops and deploys targeted digital advertising to the customer segment concerned about the issue and to relevant platforms in geographic areas in which the issue garnered the most attention. The result is targeted customers are satisfied by the the enterprise's responsiveness, prompting detractors on social media to reverse their positions and speak positively of the enterprise. Media coverage is limited and neutral in tone. A potentially problematic situation is quickly defused.

The CCO is strongly positioned to identify relevant big data opportunities and integrate data analytics into a DES. Traditional communication skill sets and leadership competencies remain vitally important—particularly given growing societal concerns regarding data privacy and security. Enterprises are learning that they have to be very thoughtful about internal and external stakeholder perceptions of how data are being gathered and used to create value. The CCO is well suited to help an enterprise navigate the risks and opportunities associated with big data models.

Mining data at scale to better understand behaviors, creating direct channels, platforms, and content to leverage predictive data insights, and engaging individuals to shape desired outcomes are the building blocks of a DES and part of the core digital playbook of successful 21st-century enterprises. Led by the CCO, these tools and techniques unlock new ways of driving customer acquisition and engagement; employee recruitment, retention, and engagement; and stakeholder influence and reputation management. It is not surprising that 55 percent of business leaders say better integrating social media with other existing digital platforms and developing an integrated digital content strategy are top strategic priorities (The Altimeter Group July 28, 2015).

Making It Happen

While DESs present enormous opportunities, the reality is that enterprises today are at various stages of readiness. Social media and digital tools may feel ubiquitous in our lives. However, while many enterprises are embracing digital trends and driving innovation, many others are grappling with the fundamentals. Efforts to utilize digital engagement are nascent. There are turf battles over who "owns" social and digital platforms. Senior management buy-in and resource commitments can be a challenge. Digital initiatives are often siloed, making cross-functional collaboration and integration of successful approaches challenging at best.

Consider this: The Altimeter Group (July 28, 2015) says that only 27 percent of enterprises surveyed report active social engagement by their executives, and only 9 percent report active C-Suite participation. That is both a problem and an opportunity. The largest single reported factor in an enterprise's social media success is C-Suite buy-in, which often requires a cultural change both at the top and throughout the enterprise (Pulse Point Group 2012).

Creating an effective DES means more than adopting social media tools and techniques. It requires:

1. Enterprise strategy and C-Suite integration;
2. Creation of data analytics and behavioral science capabilities;
3. A well-vetted brand strategy that influences social content;
4. Processes for enterprisewide governance, collaboration, design, production, and innovation.

The traditional core skills, competencies, and leadership attributes of the successful CCO make the role uniquely suited to overcoming enterprise challenges and driving digital integration, engagement, and strategy at the enterprise level.

Building a DES Begins with the Basics

Step One: Establish the Fundamentals

We propose the following framework to assess your enterprise's starting point and determine its strategic path forward. It consists of 10 fundamental questions:

1. Is there an enterprise-level social/digital *strategy*? If not, do clearly defined social/digital strategies exist within various functions, such as marketing, sales, customer service, human resources, or communication?
2. What are current digital engagement *capabilities* across the enterprise?
    (a) How are social media and digital *platforms* being used today, if at all? Identify social media channels, platforms, and monitoring tools. Is all relevant functionality of existing technology platforms being utilized? If not, why? Prioritize use cases and identify best practices.
    (b) Does the enterprise have *data analytics* capabilities? If so, where do these skills and responsibilities reside? What is the primary business purpose of data analytics? What data sets is the enterprise collecting? What is measured, by whom, and why?
    (c) How are social media and digital *structured*? One owner? Multiple? Centralized or decentralized? Discrete efforts, or cross-functional and collaborative? Do social/digital governance policies and practices exist? Are they considered effective? Do they need to be updated? Have they been communicated on a regular basis to internal stakeholders and shared with agency partners?
3. Is the C-Suite actively *engaged* in social? If not, why? Are leaders enterprisewide actively engaged? If not, why?

4. How does the enterprise currently *monitor* the perceived strength of its reputation? Is a focus on reputation management integrated into existing social/digital monitoring programs and content strategies?

5. What are the social media/digital skills and *capabilities* of the communication team? How is content created and managed? Are new roles needed, or can skill gaps be addressed through training?

6. How does the enterprise's social media/digital presence *compare* to key competitors? To influential stakeholders?

7. Does the enterprise have a *plan* for a crisis that can unfold or exacerbate in social channels? An inappropriate tweet or client issue explodes into a social media firestorm; what is the social media crisis plan?

8. Does the enterprise have a defined DES approach to *measuring* the effectiveness of digital engagement? For example, is there a standardized dashboard, updated regularly, that includes pulse checks on reputation and brand drivers, plus other stakeholder metrics derived from social media engagement and other content channels?

9. How is *content* currently created and distributed? Is there a systematic process in place? Are data analytics used to inform content? How is the effectiveness of content measured? Is content personalized and customized, or is it "one size fits all?"

10. Is a consistent communication planning and content development *process* used to prioritize relevant business objectives, identify target audiences, define desired actions and behaviors, and measure results?

Completing this or similar DES assessment frameworks is important to establish the starting point for the enterprise by understanding existing strategies, skills and capabilities, and technology assets. These insights are essential to the next step: building a business case.

Step Two: Building a Business Case to Develop a DES

By definition, a DES requires a comprehensive, holistic approach to addressing the strategic needs of the enterprise. Such a system is collaborative and cross-functional, data driven, and technology supported.

Effectively managing such an ecosystem requires a horizontal mindset and a highly coordinated, aligned, and integrative approach.

The CCO is the optimal facilitator of this process—the enterprise champion, leader, and ideal business owner of the DES. Creating and implementing a DES at scale taps the CCO's traditional reputation management expertise, the ability to see and link opportunities horizontally across the enterprise, to think outside-in, and to align diverse constituencies into a coherent strategy.

This is building authentic advocacy at scale in the digital age. Often, the CCO may share this responsibility with peers in the C-Suite, most likely the CMO, requiring collaboration and clarity of lines of responsibility and accountability.

Here is a suggested five-point approach to building the business case for a DES:

1. *Develop strategic rationales for a* DES. What business problem(s) will such a system help address? What business value will it create? Will this system facilitate and scale existing engagement strategies, or address emerging business challenges and opportunities? How will measurement occur?

2. *Identify required resources (people and technology).* This must include the four core elements of a DES: (1) data analytics capabilities; (2) the tools and skills of an effective content strategy; (3) appropriate technology channels and platforms; and (4) the necessary listening, editorial/creative, engagement, and technology skills.

3. *Determine pilot initiatives.* An effective pilot program should encompass the attributes of a strong DES. It should address: a comprehensive need of the enterprise (not a discrete issue), collaboration and integration across disciplines, data-driven insights, and measurable outcomes. Pilot initiatives are an ideal opportunity to drive C-Suite partnerships and sponsorship, and to model collaborative, cross-functional leadership.

4. *Identify and engage partners across the business.* Of relevant internal and external stakeholders—customers, investors, employees, suppliers, and regulators—who in the enterprise already may be managing digital outreach activities to these people? Tap colleagues throughout

the enterprise to understand their needs, current practices, and opportunities for collaboration.

5. *Engage the C-Suite.* As previously noted, C-Suite engagement is a critical component of success. While obviously important from a resource perspective, C-Suite support also is essential to model appropriate behaviors across the enterprise. A DES is a 21st-century business tool, designed to create competitive advantage and business value for the entire enterprise. The C-Suite must embrace it in this way.

Step Three: Test, Learn, Refine, Adapt, Measure, and Evolve

A DES, like any system, gets smarter and more robust through testing, learning, refining, and adapting. So it is important to get started. Experience and scale drive an effective DES.

Adopting a "systems" approach requires a new way of thinking for communication professionals. It moves us beyond simply creating great content and pushing it through the right channels or placing it with the right media. It means adapting traditional skill sets based on the predictive insights derived from data. It means understanding the key moments of engagement that drive behavioral change and create desired actions. It means continuously mining data. It means leveraging data, channels, and content in a systematic way to activate the enterprise's corporate character and authentic advocacy at scale.

Data are an economic asset, and a DES enables the CCO to unlock this asset, creating value for the enterprise. This can translate into an enterprise with (1) a stronger employee brand, more productive employees, and lower attrition; (2) more targeted media engagement; (3) more integrated alignment with the product, marketing, sales, and customer service strategies of the enterprise; (4) the ability to effectively influence at scale stakeholder advocacy on behalf of the enterprise; and (5) greater competitive advantage for the overall reputation and brand of the enterprise.

Summary

In a globally connected digital world, building and managing a dedicated DES is emerging as a central role of the 21st-century Communication function, and a primary responsibility of the new CCO. As noted, this nascent trend not only builds on traditional skill sets and strengths of the CCO, but also pushes us in new directions and broadens the boundaries of the modern Communication function. Data analytics, behavioral science insights, stakeholder-centric content strategies, deep digital acumen, and other skills and capabilities must be developed to capitalize on the opportunities ahead.

Leading CCOs and enterprises are embracing these changes and driving rapid innovation. The trends discussed here are reshaping how enterprises operate, compete, and grow in a digitally connected, platform-powered, technology-driven world. Leaders in all areas are grappling with these disruptive changes. From marketing and sales, to human resources and product development, leaders are learning how to adapt to this new environment, leverage emerging capabilities, and lead their enterprises forward in ways that create new value.

For all 21st-century CCOs, such action and leadership are imperative.

CHAPTER 9

Skills and Capabilities of the Modern CCO

Mark Bain, W. Timothy Coombs, and Bob Feldman

The nature and practice of all work continually evolves.

Today, for example, many products are designed in three dimensions on sophisticated software, rather than in two dimensions on paper draped over a large drafting table. These products are manufactured by precise robots in highly automated factories, with smaller numbers of less efficient and consistent humans playing more of a secondary role. Many of these products are then marketed and purchased online, with overnight delivery enabled by private carriers whose enormous fleets operate in a complex, closely synchronized ballet of logistics.

The nature and practice of communication has changed dramatically in recent years, as well. New technology tools, more globally integrated markets, and other factors have altered much of what communicators do and how we do it. The scale and pace of some change in our field has been profound.

Not so long ago, enterprises practiced mostly one-way, top-down communication. To inform and persuade masses of stakeholders, the CCO's tools included news releases, advertisements, brochures, newsletters, and the like. Although these tools are still in use, they have taken on different forms and often are distributed in different ways. News releases are now primarily digital and distributed instantly across social and digital platforms, both shared and owned. Online ads target specific stakeholders based on their uniquely individual interests and preferences, and brochures and newsletters are increasingly shared in digital, not printed, form via e-mail, Internet, or intranet.

Contemporary social and digital platforms have allowed for more two-way, interactive and real-time exchanges between the enterprise and its diverse stakeholder constituencies (see Chapters 5 and 8). This has gone well beyond mere awareness to building greater engagement, belief, confidence, trust, and advocacy.

At the same time, dramatic changes in communication tools and processes have led to changing expectations of when, how, and where an enterprise and its stakeholders will engage. And new tools have required communicators, including CCOs, to develop broader and more balanced skill sets.

With communication becoming more of a management function with C-Suite status, CCOs are expected to be proficient in more than just communication. Legacy skills, including writing and presenting, remain fundamentally important. At the same time, CCOs are expected to have the *right* sets of interpersonal skills to collaborate with colleagues and engage both friendly and hostile stakeholders, while being adroit at managing and leading teams that are often dispersed and virtual. The CCO is expected to have the business acumen and operational and organizational savvy to move work forward, even in a VUCA (volatile, uncertain, changing, and ambiguous) environment.

Most of all, CCOs (and the expert consultants who advise and support them) are expected to deliver tangible, measurable, and sustainable business value to the enterprise, not just bigger and better communication results.

With this and prior chapters as a backdrop, and as part of the Arthur W. Page Society's *New CCO* (Arthur W. Page Society 2016) research, a working group of Page members identified three broad sets of skills and capabilities required for the new CCO:

1. *Communication skills*, which involve mastery of written and oral communication skill coupled with metrics that provide feedback and actionable insights;
2. *Interpersonal skills*, which reflect the growing emphasis on collaboration along with the emotional intelligence required for working effectively with others inside and outside the enterprise; and
3. *Management and leadership skills*, which align and marshal in-house and external communication resources to perform at ever-higher levels and deliver greater business value.

These three sets of skills and capabilities are the key points to be addressed in this chapter. After each has been addressed, a case study demonstrates how the three skill sets were used when a new CCO took the reins of the enterprise's communication function.

Communication Skills

Writing and presenting effectively are still fundamental to effective communication (Daft and Marcic 2013). An elevated ability to clearly and persuasively express a point of view, either orally or in writing, is essential for communicators at every level, including the CCO, who often is expected to create mission-critical talking points, position papers, statements, CEO memos, speeches, presentations, and the like. A CCO must also have a keen understanding of how to communicate across different cultures and media, from 140-character tweets to lengthy speeches on major policy positions.

CCOs must have strong skills around metrics *and* reporting. As with any enterprise corporate function, communication must prove its worth with relevant metrics, ideally correlated to business outcomes, not just communication processes. Perhaps more important, with data generated by social and digital media (see Chapter 8), CCOs and their teams have powerful tools to get visibility and insight into the thoughts, beliefs, and actions of key stakeholders. In fact, the granularity of data today allows CCOs to focus on audience segments, or even down to the individual, in a retroactive, real-time, or prospective manner. Social media are often noted as a source for early indication of potential issues; mining those conversations, filtering the signal from the noise, interpreting the impact, and anticipating a broader issue are hallmarks of the modern communication function. This ability underscores the need for CCOs to have competency with data analytics.

Several other technical skills reflect specific applications of strategic communication: corporate positioning, issues/crisis management, strategic media relations, and internal communication.

Corporate positioning emphasizes the need for enterprises to differentiate themselves by identifying and conveying the distinctiveness of the enterprise.

Issues and crisis management help the enterprise to identify and manage risks in a highly networked and volatile world. We will see the application of issues management in a case study looking at Andeavor (formerly Tesoro), a Texas-based Fortune 100 enterprise through the engagement of external stakeholders (also known as environmental scanning).

Strategic media relations moves past basic publicity to an understanding of how media relations can be used to achieve enterprise goals. In a crisis, for instance, strategic media relations can help an enterprise disseminate information, advance its position, protect its reputation, and retain stakeholder trust through a small number of timely, well-placed stories.

Internal communication has grown in importance as significant percentages of employees in all industries and regions have become disengaged in enterprise corporate strategic priorities (c.f., Men and Bowen 2017). Effective internal communication can enhance strategy implementation, increase retention of top talent, and serve as a valuable asset during a crisis.

A significant body of research has developed around the idea of corporate positioning. Of particular note is the evolving way that CCOs are leading their enterprises to think about corporate social responsibility (CSR). Early CSR programs were sometimes tactical in nature, involving checkbook philanthropy and one-off programs to generate vague levels of goodwill, perhaps to offset certain negative elements of the business (Becker-Olsen, Cudmore, and Hill 2006; Srinaruewan, Binney, and Higgins 2015). More recently, CSR has evolved into a fuller communication and business strategy built around the enterprise's "social purpose"—the value that it delivers to society and all stakeholders, beyond its customer or shareholder value (Srinaruewan et al. 2015). Social purpose is a powerful driver of stakeholder engagement.

As noted in Chapter 4, in the Page Model, social purpose is central to corporate character—the vision, mission, values, and beliefs that comprise the foundation of any enterprise (Arthur W. Page Society 2012a). Clear purpose allows a CCO to forge shared belief with stakeholders, foster confidence, move them to action, and earn their trust and advocacy. The key is for COOs to help identify, articulate, and align purpose across business and communication. Here, skills in strategic planning, partnership building, and persuasion—ideally built on insightful data—are complementary.

Crisis management is a skill that both professionals and academics recognize as increasing in importance over the past decade. More specifically, both groups recognize the value of effective crisis communication to an enterprise. Research has shown the value of effective crisis communication for protecting institutional assets such reputation and purchase intention. The choice of crisis response strategies has a demonstrable effect on stakeholder perceptions of the enterprise's reputation, likelihood to engage in negative word-of-mouth, and purchase intentions (Coombs and Holladay 2002, 2005). One interesting finding is that enterprises suffer less reputation damage when it is the *first* source to report the existence of a crisis (Arpan and Pompper 2003; Claeys and Cauberghe 2012). Moreover, research has defined how effective responses can vary from crisis to crisis. Demonstrating concern for stakeholders affected by the crisis as part of the crisis response is an enduring element of effective crisis communication (e.g., Coombs 2007).

Interpersonal Skills

In addition to mastery of technical communication skills, effective and well-rounded CCOs have a varying set of interpersonal skills that enable them to connect with others, gain support, and move work forward.

Sometimes referred to as "soft" skills, interpersonal skills are anything but soft in their importance to the modern enterprise. The Page working group identified nine complementary skills and capabilities in this area divided into three groups: (1) core skills, (2) change-related skills, and (3) other-focused skills. These three groups reflect different challenges communicators face in seeking to be enterprise leaders.

The core skill sets are comprised of listening, collaborating, and relating with senior management.

Listening is like air and water—essential in any position and especially in leadership roles (Harrison and Mülhberg 2014). Listening takes place throughout our daily interactions. Leaders must understand the thoughts and feelings of those inside and outside the enterprise. Without such understanding, it will be virtually impossible to find common ground, build trust, elevate engagement, and activate advocacy (Matin, Jandaghi, Karimi, and Hamidizadeh 2010).

Collaboration has become more important as enterprises have grown larger, more complex, and more diverse. Even simple communication work—a news release, for example—can require the review and approval of multiple functions, including legal (CLO or general counsel), finance (CFO), marketing (CMO), human resources (CHRO), information technology (CIO), and, often, the CEO. A larger, multifaceted change management initiative could enlist heavy ongoing engagement across the C-Suite. In the global enterprise, collaboration takes on an added geographic dimension on top of the functional element. Most large international enterprises now operate in a highly matrixed manner, so CCOs and their team members must work productively with others.

To optimize collaboration, CCOs must be especially adept at *relating with senior management*. Listening and compassion are aspects of this ability to relate to others, as are understanding how senior leaders think and how the business works. On occasion, CCOs will be required to "speak truth to power," sharing unwelcome information and/or advocating an approach that challenges existing positions but may ultimately be in the best interests of the enterprise. An ability to effectively persuade the CEO and other business leaders in a constructive manner can cement the CCO's role as a trusted adviser and integral part of the senior leadership team.

The *change-related skills* reflect the rapidly changing enterprise environment. The change-related skills include: (1) dealing with ambiguity, (2) change management, and (3) drive for results (Matos Marques Simoes and Esposito 2014).

Turbulent environments create ambiguity and uncertainty, wherein it becomes harder to predict how stakeholders will behave, what competitors might do, and how regulators might act. Communication leaders can add business value by bringing clarity to the ambiguity that surrounds it while participating in managing the change that results from disruption and other factors.

Communicators are increasingly involved in change management not only because communication itself is an intrinsically important element, but also because CCOs are expanding their capabilities to include change management theory, principles, and practices.

A drive for results is another trait that matters more in a time when agile start-ups are disrupting industries and stealing share from slower enterprise behemoths. CEOs are under pressure from impatient boards, shareholders, and other stakeholders to drive growth and deliver profits. One-hundred-day plans are now the *norm* for new leaders to show tangible progress—or else. In this environment, CCOs must be more nimble, agile, and progressive—or else.

This same Page working group cited three *other-focused skills* as central: (1) compassion, (2) mentor and coach, and (3) inspiring and motivating others.

Communication leaders must be sensitive to *all* enterprise stakeholders. Frequently, CCOs interact with people who challenge their employer's positions and actions. *Compassion*, in combination with effective listening, enhances understanding, facilitates resolution, and converts adversaries into advocates for the mutual benefit of all parties.

Mentoring and coaching prepares the next generation of leaders and fulfills individual needs for growth by improving skills. As boards and CEOs expect more from all of their functions, including communication, CCOs will need to attract and retain high-performing talent to deliver value. Mentoring and coaching talent within their teams will help CCOs achieve that goal (Sanchez-Cortes, Aran, Jayagopi, Mast, and Gatica-Perez 2013).

Inspiring and motivating others goes hand-in-hand with mentoring and coaching. There is truth to the adage that people work for leaders, not for enterprises. A weak leader in a great enterprise might initially attract top talent, but will have a difficult time retaining them. An inspiring and motivating CCO who brings out the best in everyone will keep top performers and attract other strong talent, elevating the value she or he brings to the enterprise.

Management/Leadership Skills

The Page working group on *the New CCO* (2016) identified seven management/leadership skills that seem especially relevant in the current environment: business acumen, strategic business thinking, problem solving, managing character, running effective teams, courageous counsel, and taking leadership.

Business acumen. From literature and commentary, there appears to be growing support that a strong understanding of how the business works is just as important, if not more important, than other communication and interpersonal skills. At a minimum, communication skills are described as *table stakes*—the price of entry (Korn Ferry Institute 2015). There is more to business acumen than understanding a financial balance sheet. CCOs must have a thorough understanding of how the enterprise generates revenues, manages costs, and produces profits. In addition, CCOs must understand how their enterprise develops, makes, prices, and distributes its products; how it applies responsible practices across the enterprise and throughout the supply chain; how it treats all stakeholders, including policies and practices for union and nonunion employees; how technology enables the business and how personal privacy and data security are preserved; how legislators and regulators view the enterprise's industry; how competitors differ; and more. A promising communication program that does not conform with the financial and operating realities of the enterprise will remain just that—promising.

Strategic business thinking. Many CCOs have a seat at table as full C-Suite members, or at least observers, on their enterprise's senior leadership team. They are expected to demonstrate not just subject matter expertise (e.g., communication skills), but a broad understanding of the entire business so they may advise on business matters in general and crisis and reputation matters in particular (see Chapter 4; Harrison and Mülberg 2014).

Problem solving. Increasingly, CEOs turn to members of the C-Suite to solve business problems and seize opportunities anywhere in the enterprise, regardless of their functional expertise. CCOs with business acumen and a strategic mind for business problems and opportunities become indispensable to the management teams and enterprise. The CCO's ability to think across enterprise functions and to plan strategic communication plans and responses adds an intangible value to the C-Suite. As the CEO's primary communication strategist, the CCO can develop a close working relationships with the CEO.

Managing corporate character. Because stakeholder trust depends on what enterprises do, not just what they say, the foundations of enterprise corporate character as discussed in Chapter 4—mission, vision, values, and so forth—must be clearly understood and optimally activated to encourage stakeholder support (Men and Tsai 2015; Moore 2015). CCOs are well positioned to lead in this area because of their panoramic view of enterprise culture and interactions with stakeholders of all types.

Running effective teams. In this era of high collaboration, cross-functional and global teams are often the mechanism to develop ideas, build support, drive change, and advance corporate strategies (Wheelan 2014). The CCO and communicators at all levels should have the organizational savvy and process management skills to play leading roles on these teams. An effective team is one that takes in data, analyzes it, evaluates it, and then interprets it for C-Suite discussion. An effective communication team will be asked to participate in strategic discussions, not simply announce them.

Courageous counsel. Communication leaders must be willing to speak regardless of whether others will like what they have to say—or perhaps especially when they will not. Being courageous and speaking out are an essential element to being a trusted and valuable strategic adviser. Clearly, however, the CCO must understand enterprise culture, carefully listening and scanning the enterprise for problems and being proactive in managing them. Simply stated, the CCO is a proactive strategist, thinking both inside and outside the box.

Taking leadership. A growing number of CEOs want solutions and are agnostic about their origin. Anyone in the C-Suite is invited to pitch in on a thorny problem and drive a promising opportunity. This capability requires confidence and initiative, volunteering to assume responsibility for matters that are of the highest importance to the enterprise. To be seen as trusted advisers and valued contributors to the business, CCOs should step up and take leadership roles where their panoramic, multistakeholder perspective will add value. They must take ownership and clearly articulate their positions with hard data and a deep evaluation and clear interpretation of things inside and outside the enterprise.

Finally, CCOs must possess the skills required to design, build, and implement processes and systems. In the past, when the function's primary rule was to provide communications services to the enterprise, this skill may have been less important. But as detailed in the Page Society paper, *The CCO as Builder of Digital Engagement Systems*, the CCO now has an opportunity to build and deploy systems that monitor stakeholder conversations, create and share relevant content, and engage stakeholders (Arthur W. Page Society 2016).

The following case illustrates the evolution of work and many of the skills and capabilities required of modern CCOs presented in this chapter.[1]

Case: Putting Skill Sets into Practice

Upgrading the Andeavor Communication Function

When Greg Goff became Andeavor's CEO in 2010, there were concerns about the enterprise's future. The enterprise needed to take bold steps, quickly, to improve its competitiveness and prepare for future growth.[2]

Goff made it an early priority to strengthen his senior leadership team [C-Suite], reasoning that higher performance required the right people to drive operational and cultural change. New senior leaders, in turn, brought additional talent into their respective functions, including Corporate Communication, a catalyst for internal and external stakeholder engagement.

Following an industry downturn, Andeavor's communication function lacked the talent needed for a large enterprise in a highly regulated and often contentious environment. The function was also unprepared to contribute to Andeavor's ambitious growth plans. Communication work was largely reactive, and the function's relationships—internally

---

[1] This case was prepared by Mark Bain with the help of Jill M. Saletta, vice president for Corporate Communication at Andeavor.

[2] Tesoro Corporation (NYSE: TSO aka: "Tesoro Petroleum," or simply as "Tesoro") is a Fortune 100[5] and a Fortune Global 500 company headquartered in Texas at San Antonio, with 2013 annual revenues of $37 billion, and over 5,700 employees worldwide. Tesoro is an independent refiner and marketer of petroleum products, operating seven refineries in the Western United States with a combined rated crude oil capacity of approximately 845,000 barrels (134,300 m^3) per day. Tesoro's retail-marketing system includes over 2,264 branded retail gas stations, of which more than 595 are company-operated under its own Tesoro brand name, as well as Shell, ExxonMobil, ARCO, and USA Gasoline brands.

with business leaders, and externally with key stakeholders—needed to deepen.

Jill Saletta was hired as Andeavor's CCO, or formally vice president of Corporate Communication, in 2011. Reflecting Goff's approach, she quickly developed a three-year strategy to increase external visibility and improve employee engagement. Both would lay the foundation for more robust reputation management and stakeholder engagement efforts to come.

Aligning the Team and Business

Early on, Saletta saw that her function was not aligned with the business, in part because her group did not possess the skills to perform as trusted counselors and valued business partners. In line with her three-year strategy, Saletta brought on generalists with strong writing and relationship-building skills. These generalists were able to straddle internal and external communication, flexing focus whenever demand shifted. She also drove alignment within her team through new or improved processes, such as a Monday morning production meeting to set priorities and allocate work.

Creating a Shared Vision

With the right talent in place, Saletta then turned to developing a more cohesive and aligned team.

First, she invited all of her team members to collaborate in crafting a *shared vision* for the function (see Chapter 4). The resulting vision statement, which all had a hand in writing, clarified the team's primary role ("build and protect corporate reputation"), explained how it worked ("trusted advisers and valued partners"), and set forth what it aspired to become ("leading team").

To achieve this vision, the group developed a set of 18 initial values unique to the function and complementary to the enterprise's values. These values defined the behaviors expected from communication team members at every level. Examples of their values included:

- Business acumen
- Gravitas
- Tenacity
- Discipline

Specifying Skill Sets and Competencies

Finally, the group selected specific skills and competencies needed to better serve the business. It settled upon 19 critical skills in three broad clusters—*communication skills, interpersonal skills, and management/leadership skills*. These were incorporated into the enterprise's standardized performance management process and the function's professional development planning to monitor and measure progress.

"Aspire"

The vision, values, and competencies were captured and expressed in a unique "operating system" the team called Aspire. This system brought the values and competencies to life through a collective set of commitments for how Andeavor's Corporate Communication function would develop team members and manage, measure, and reward performance. The system was shared with existing team members as an interactive PDF, and is now given to new hires when they join.

Summary

Saletta says these efforts have helped her team increase its capabilities and expand its capacity. As the team has mastered several of its initial 19 skills, it has started to look at new ones to add. The initial 18 values have been instrumental in setting and managing expectations for behaviors, and the vision statement will soon be updated as the Corporate Communication role expands.

More important, these efforts have elevated the team's performance and, with it, its stature in the enterprise. Several internal clients now see Corporate Communication as one of the enterprise's high-performing teams. Demand for communicators to have regular involvement in the business has risen dramatically, and some communication team members have even been borrowed (full-time, in some instances) by enterprisewide teams working on major corporate initiatives.

This comprehensive and disciplined approach to clarifying direction and setting ever-higher performance standards has helped the Andeavor Corporate Communication team shift from a reactive to proactive stance, with growing expertise not just in executing communication tactics but, increasingly, in providing advice and solutions for critical business matters.

(Note Andeavor's name was changed from Tesoro following an acquisition effective August 1, 2017).

Bringing It All Together

It is critical for CCOs to be multidimensional, well rounded, and balanced in all three of these skill sets. A CCO who is a strong communicator but less proficient in other areas will enjoy less influence in the C-Suite. Likewise, a CCO who is not a strong manager and leader will struggle to attract and retain the top talent needed to drive optimal business value, lessening her/his impact on the business.

For many years, some communicators were elevated into the CCO role largely based on their expertise in all forms of communication. Looking ahead, communication skills alone will be insufficient to drive the business outcomes CEOs want and expect from the enterprise Corporate Communication function.

CHAPTER 10

The New Reality

Roger Bolton, Jennifer Prosek, and Don W. Stacks

The role of the chief communication officer (CCO) has changed dramatically over the last half-century. Previously, it was a *tactical function*, focused on what might be called "push" communication—where the goal was to create awareness and understanding by taking information generated by others in the enterprise and passing it on to the appropriate stakeholder constituency. There was little strategy, little formal research, and the role exemplified what Broom and colleagues (1982; Broom and Dozier 1986; Broom and Smith 1979) labeled "technician." Public relations was seen as a way get free publicity and outcomes were often defined as the size of the clipbook from generated media pick-ups. Today, however, the communication function has become a *strategic function* in the enterprise. Rather than simply writing executive speeches, media releases, or internal newsletters, the function now leads the enterprise's *strategic positioning* and *stakeholder engagement*. Instead of being reactive and one-way, the communication function is now proactive and interactive. The CCO and her staff take both an inside–outside and outside–inside 360° strategic look at the enterprise and its corporate character. Instead of being a function "off to the side," it is now deeply embedded in the C-Suite as a strategic partner.

The New Chief Communication Officer

As the enterprise has transformed over the past few decades, so too has the CCO's role. This change, motivated first by globalization, social media, and stakeholder empowerment, forced the enterprise to take a broader approach to dealing with a new world order: Almost everyone who wanted to could engage with it for good or bad via social media, confirming the importance of the two-way symmetrical channel (Grunig 1987). Any stakeholder—active, aware, inactive, or latent—could now get his or her voice into the mix. Further adding to the enterprise's transformation were shifts in geopolitics and demographics, which, in turn, added new, disruptive business models and a changing of the nature of work in general; and the stakeholder shifted from being empowered to actually becoming an active force in the enterprise's business plans. The resulting change in the role of the CCO is described in the Page Model, shown in Figure 10.1. Here we see the CCO's new focus starting with the enterprise's corporate character (Arthur W. Page Society 2007). The CCO now helps the enterprise define, activate, and align its mission, vision, values, culture, business model, strategy, and brand. This is a significant departure from the old model, where the CCO waited for

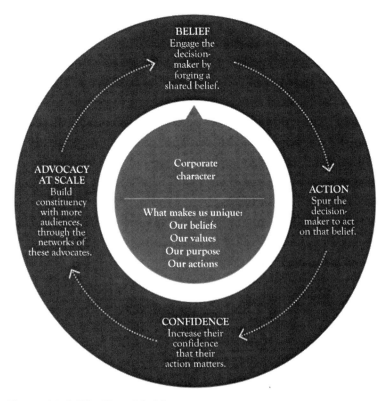

Figure 10.1 The Page Model

others to make decisions and then sought to explain them to stakeholders. Now, the CCO takes an active role in encouraging and sometimes leading the enterprise's definition of its essential identity. In short, an enterprise that wishes to be trusted first must make itself trustworthy, and that has become job one for the CCO.

This central assumption—that enterprise identity is a function of its corporate character—then provides the foundation upon which a trusting relationship can be built with stakeholders. The model suggests that the first step is to establish shared belief; that is, to find a core of agreement between the company's true character and the beliefs of the stakeholder. For example, the company and the stakeholder may mutually agree that the company should be environmentally responsible. A conversation can then occur, with both sides listening and being willing to change, on the details of exactly what the company is doing and what it should be expected to do. Once shared belief is achieved, a stakeholder may be motivated to take an action, such as buying a product or the stock, supporting a policy objective, or entering into a partnership of some sort. This may or may not involve a change in policy or perspective from either or both of the parties. If the action is repeated and each side begins to gain confidence in the other, the stakeholder may begin to feel aligned enough with the organization to become an advocate. That advocacy across a wide set of stakeholder constituencies can lead to more shared belief with additional stakeholders, and the virtuous cycle begins anew.

So, if the Page Model shows *what* the modern CCO must do, the question remains *how* she can do it, and the answer to that—outlined in *The New CCO* report—also represents a major change from the past. We have identified through earlier chapters three critical roles the CCO must play to ensure enterprise success. First, there is the "foundational role" described in Chapter 6—strategic business counselor, steward of enterprise reputation, effective communicator, and builder of stakeholder relationships. Second, there is the "integrator role" as demonstrated in Chapter 7, in which the CCO encourages or leads cross-functional teams within the C-Suite that build corporate character and stakeholder engagement. And, third, in what is clearly the newest and most aspirational role, the CCO of the future will be a builder of digital engagement systems (DESs). This role, as described in Chapter 8, brings the CCO full strategic authority to create information models that can be used across enterprise functions via the massive accumulation of data—both hard and soft (see Stacks 2017)—to build authentic, two-way relationships with stakeholders and to engage all employees in that effort.

The Role of the CCO

In sum, the role of the CCO can be understood this way:

- The primary job is to build and defend brand and reputation because this earns permission to operate and gives the enterprise the support it needs to implement its strategy and fulfill its purpose. The CCO does this by:

  1. Working within the enterprise to build corporate character, which is the unique differentiating identity of the organization, defined by mission, purpose, values, culture, business model, strategy, and brand.
  2. Building stakeholder engagement that results in advocacy.

- In order to do these things, the CCO has three roles:

  1. **The foundational role**—strategic business counselor, steward of enterprise reputation, effective communicator, and builder of stakeholder relationships.
  2. **The integrator role**—using leadership skills, the CCO works across the enterprise to build allies in the definition and activation of corporate character and stakeholder engagement.
  3. **The builder of DESs**, which require new skills and capabilities to authentically engage internal and external stakeholders.

What's Next?

The pace of change described in Chapters 1 to 3 is unlikely to abate. If anything, it appears to be accelerating. The challenges facing our world are immense and growing, despite significant and undeniable progress.

It has been more than 70 years since the end of the last world war and the Cold War was ended more than a quarter-century ago. Yet, regional and tribal conflicts, terrorism, and rogue nuclear states make peace on earth a distant dream. Extreme poverty has been halved over the past 25 years and hundreds of millions of people in developing countries have entered the middle class, yet growing income inequality and stagnation in developed countries are creating a sense of unfairness, hopelessness, and political conflict that threatens the existence of the multilateral postwar world order. The pace of technological change holds out breathtaking promise for human advancement in knowledge, connection, efficiency, and well-being, but at the same time threatens disruption of existing businesses and employment and creates risks to privacy, economic security, and even worries about our future in a world of artificially intelligent machines.

In the face of these challenges, and others not yet imagined, we believe strongly in the power of business to be a force for good in the world—not alone, but in partnership with governments and nongovernmental organizations (NGOs). Of the three sectors, business is unique because its economic model is self-sustaining and it is most likely to create innovative new solutions to the world's problems. We believe business is more likely to play a positive role in society when it has a strong CCO whose focus is on creating a corporate character based on a social-value-creating purpose and an ethical set of values that guide its actions. The CCO is most likely to be focused on stakeholder engagement, which requires listening and responsiveness to the needs of the world. Governments and NGOs also play a key role with each sector holding the others accountable and working cooperatively to create the conditions to advance economic and social value and justice.

As the world evolves and new challenges and opportunities emerge, the role of the CCO will continue to evolve, as well. We predict that corporate communication will continue to be a strategic function within the enterprise and will not return to its more tactical, order-taking role of the past. CCOs will continue to act as senior leaders in the enterprise, sharing responsibility for the strategy and success of the enterprise with their counterparts across the C-Suite. The adaptability and willingness to take on new skills and capabilities that CCOs have shown in the past, while staying focused on the enduring truths expressed in the Page Principles and the Page Model, will benefit both our profession and the enterprises we serve in the days and years to come.

In his foreword, Dave Sampson opens with a quote from the Greek philosopher Heraclitus: "There is nothing permanent, except change." In this new world where truth is a luxury, stakeholders can activate a movement overnight, and reputations can be lost in seconds, the role of the CCO has become a critical, high-stakes position where change is constant and permanent. The communication function has been permanently reframed. CCOs of today and into the future will need a new level of fortitude, morality, and skills to help their enterprises navigate an extremely complex world. They will need to embrace change and be vigorous with their own continuous learning. They will need to have a higher level of conviction, energy, emotional intelligence, and technical savvy than ever before. The role, for certain, will become more challenging. But, also for certain, the work will be among the most rewarding, important, and impactful of any C-level profession.

References

2030 Water Resources Group. 2009. *Charting Our Water Future*. McKinsey & Company. http://mckinsey.com/business-functions/sustainability-and-resource-productivity/our-insights/charting-our-water-future

3p Contributor. September 25, 2015. "Why Businesses Should Care About Water Security." *Triple Pundit*. http://triplepundit.com/2015/09/businesses-care-water-security/#

Ad Age. June 17, 2015. Best Practices: How to Create a Rewards Program that Really Works. http://adage.com/article/cmo-strategy/practices-create-a-rewards-program-works/299018/

Andreessen, M. August 20, 2011. "Why Software is Eating the World." *Wall Street Journal*. http://wsj.com/articles/SB10001424053111903480904576512250915629460

Argenti, P. March 23, 2016. "Developing A One Company Culture: The Key to Aligning Strategy with Execution." Retrieved May 14, 2016.

Argenti, P.A. 2016. *Corporate Communication*, 7th ed. New York: McGraw Hill Education.

Argenti, P.A., and C.B. Van Riel. n.d. "Developing a One-Company Culture." Retrieved May 1, 2016.

Arpan, L.M., and D. Pompper. 2003. "Stormy Weather: Testing 'stealing Thunder' as a Crisis Communication Strategy to Improve Communication Flow Between Organizations and Journalists." *Public Relations Review* 29, no. 3, pp. 291–308.

Arthur W. Page Society. n.d. *Page Society Historical Perspective*. http://awpagesociety.com/site/historical-perspective

Arthur W. Page Society. n.d. *Vision, Mission, and Goals*. http://awpagesociety.com/site/vision-misson-goals

Arthur W. Page Society. 2007. *The Authentic Enterprise*. New York: Arthur W. Page Society. http:/awpagesociety.com/site/members/page_society_releases_the_authentic_enterprise/ doi:March 7, 2016

Arthur W. Page Society. 2012a. *Building Belief: A New Model for Activating Corporate Character & Authentic Advocacy*. http://awpagesociety.com/attachments/508b442e53cd975472b3fa3f405c7c35f03cf6-Belief-New-Model-for-Corp-Comms.pdf

Arthur W. Page Society. 2012b. *The Economics of the Socially Engaged Enterprise*. New York: Arthur W. Page Society. https://slideshare.net/PulsePoint_Group/arthur-page

Arthur W. Page Society. 2013a. *Social Engagement, Part One: The Evolution of Social Media as a Business Tool.* New York: Arthur W. Page Society. http://awpagesociety.com/thought-leadership/social-engagement

Arthur W. Page Society. 2013b. *The CEO View: The Impact On Corporate Character in a 24x7 Digital World.* http://awpagesociety.com/attachments/ea66f4d21818b50a07ba131739f6276d292f3431/store/7b311aaf40c60f8d6efd541db8a53c7689258263e6600fb2031e8c39da33/The-CEO-View-2013.pdf

Arthur W. Page Society. 2013c. *The New Model: Corporate Character: How Leading Companies Are Defining, Activating & Aligning Values.* https://awpagesociety.com/attachments/01b59317a909e6b0d001436edeb8ae3c727b0643/store/275a6e4abd17b75f72f5f932847e6dbef6233b513a68829bb89b9b016a0f/Full_Report.pdf

Arthur W. Page Society. 2014. *Authentic Advocacy: How Five Leading Companies are Redefining Stakeholder Engagement.* https://docs.google.com/gview?url=https://awpagesociety.com/attachments/eacb62ad8aad3f3f8da014d0c0fc992a45893205/store/4485a27e51cdd97f67f903a5baaf3af7ca3c9063a3833f773580e41a375d/Full_Report.pdf

Arthur W. Page Society. 2016. *The New CCO: Transforming Enterprises in a Changing World.* http://awpagesociety.com/attachments/2c2ba4f62f6ec9f850bbf466eda52099ae4b5fa6/store/f6aebd3e039d0270d58b4c6bc72ae25674dd08a857f60c3c6fbcf970155f/Page+Society+-+The+New+CCO.pdf

Arthur W. Page Society. May 2017. *The CEO View: Communications as the Center of the Enterprise.* http://awpagesociety.com/thought-leadership/the-ceo-view-communications-at-the-center-of-the-enterprise

Ashforth, B.E., and F.A. Mael. 1989. "Social Identity Theory and the Organization." *Academy of Management Review* 14, no. 1, pp. 29–39.

Badgett, M.V.L., L.E. Durso, A. Kastanis, and C. Mallory. May 2013. "The Business Impact of LGBT-Supportive Workplace Policies." http://williamsinstitute.law.ucla.edu/wp-content/uploads/Business-Impact-LGBT-Policies-Full-Report-May-2013.pdf

Balmer, J.M.T., and S.A. Greyser. 2003. *Revealing the Corporation: Perspectives on Identity, Image, Reputation, Corporate Branding and Corporate-Level Marketing.* London: Routledge.

Barras, M. June 5, 2014. GM CEO Mary Barra's Remarks to Employees on Valukas Report Findings Remarks, 8–10. http://media.gm.com/media/us/en/gm/news.detail.html/content/Pages/news/us/en/2014/Jun/060514-mary-remarks.html

Becker-Olsen, K.L., B.A. Cudmore, and R.P. Hill. 2006. "The Impact of Perceived Corporate Social Responsibility on Consumer Behavior." *Journal of business research* 59, no. 1, pp. 46–53.

Berle, A. 1931. "Corporate Powers as Powers in Trust." *Harvard Law Review* 44, no. 7, 1049–74. https://harvardlawreview.org/

Block E.M. 1993. "HOF Induction Speech." http://awpagesociety.com/speeches/hall_of_fame/1993-hall-of-fame-award-acceptance-speech

Block, E.M. 2004. "Arthur W. Page: The Legacy of Public Relations Excellence Behind the Name." http://comm.psu.edu/page-assets/assets/pdf/arthur-w-page-by-block.pdf (accessed June 8, 2016).

Blowfield, M., and B.K. Googins. 2006. *Step Up: A Call for Business Leadership in Society.* Boston College Center for Corporate Citizenship. http://ccc.bc.edu/index.cfm?fuseaction=document.showDocument ByID&DocumentID=1072

Boston College Center for Corporate Citizenship. 2009. *Mapping Stakeholder Landscapes: The Influence and Impact of Global Stakeholders.* http://ccc.bc.edu/index.cfm?fuseaction=document.showDocument ByID&DocumentID=1337

Botan, C. 1997. "Ethics in Strategic Communication Campaigns: The Case for a New Approach to Public Relations." *The Journal of Business Communication* 34, no. 2, pp. 188–202.

Bowen, S.A. 2002. "Elite Executives in Issues Management: The Role of Ethical Paradigms in Decision Making." *Journal of Public Affairs* 2, no. 4, pp. 270–83.

Bowen, S.A. 2004. "Organizational Factors Encouraging Ethical Decision Making: An Exploration into the Case of an Exemplar." *Journal of Business Ethics* 52, no. 4, pp. 311–24.

Bowen, S.A. 2005. "Mission and Vision Statements." In *Encyclopedia of Public Relations,* ed. R.L. Heath, 535–37. 2 vols. Thousand Oaks, CA: Sage.

Bowen, S.A. 2008. "A State of Neglect: Public Relations as Corporate Conscience or Ethics Counsel." *Journal of Public Relations Research* 20, no. 3, pp. 271–96.

Bowen, S.A. 2009. "What Communication Professionals Tell Us Regarding Dominant Coalition Access and Gaining Membership." *Journal of Applied Communication Research* 37, no, 4, pp. 427–52.

Bowen, S.A. 2010. "Almost a Decade Later: Have We Learned Lessons from Inside the Crooked E, Enron?" *Ethical Space: The International Journal of Communication Ethics* 7, no. 1, pp. 569–83.

Bowen, S.A. 2012. "The Ethics of Pre-Crisis Communication." In *Pre-Crisis Planning, Communication, and Management: Preparing For the Inevitable,* eds. B.A. Olaniran, D.E. Williams, and W.T. Coombs, 55–78. New York, NY: Peter Lang Publishing.

Bowen, S.A. 2016. "Clarifying Ethics Terms in Public Relations from A to V, Authenticity to Virtue. BledCom Special Issue of PR Review Sleeping (with the) Media: Media Relations." *Public Relations Review.* http://dx.doi.org/10.1016/j.pubrev.2016.03.012

Bowen, S.A., and R.L. Heath. 2005. "Issues Management, Systems, and Rhetoric: Exploring the Distinction Between Ethical and Legal Guidelines at Enron." *Journal of Public Affairs* 5, no. 2, pp. 84–98.

Bowen, S.A., B. Rawlins, and T. Martin. 2010. *An Overview of the Public Relations Function*. New York, NY: Business Expert Press.

Bowen, S.A., C.J. Hung-Baesecke, and Y.R. Chen. 2016. "Ethics as a Pre-Cursor to Organization-Public Relationships: Building Trust Before and During the OPR Model." *Cogent Social Sciences* 2, no. 1. http://dx.doi.org/10.1080/233 11886.2016.1141467

Bowen, S.A., D.W. Stacks, and D.K. Wright. 2017. "Emissions Scandal: An Example of Bad Public Relations on a Worldwide Scale and the Defeat Device that Needed a Worldwide Reputation." In *Public Relations Case Studies from Around the World*, eds. J.V. Turk, J. Paluszek, and J. Valin, 3–21. 2nd ed. New York, NY: Peter Lang Publishing.

Bowen, S.A., R.L. Heath, J. Lee, G. Painter, F.J. Agraz, D. McKie, M. Toledano. 2006. *The Business of Truth: A Guide to Ethical Communication Perspective*. San Francisco: International Association of Business Communicators Research Foundation.

Broom, G.M. 1982. "A Comparison of Sex Roles in Public Relations." *Public Relations Review* 8, no. 3, pp. 17–22.

Broom, G.M., and D.M. Dozier. 1986. "Advancement for Public Relations Role Models." *Public Relations Review* 12, no. 1, pp. 37–56.

Broom, G.M., and D.M. Dozier. 1986. *Using Research in Public Relations: Applications to Program Management*. Englewood Cliffs, NJ: Prentice-Hall.

Broom, G.M., and G.D. Smith. 1979. "Testing the Practitioner's Impact on Clients." *Public Relations Review* 5, no. 3, pp. 47–59.

Burson, H. 2013. *Remarks to the Public Relations Leadership Forum*. New York Rosetta Books.

CBS News Money Watch. April 2, 2014. "Senators Accuse GM of Covering Up Defective Switch." http://cbsnews.com/news/senators-accuse-gm-of-covering-up-defective-switch/

Ceres. n.d. "Ceres (Organization)". https://en.wikipedia.org/wiki/Ceres_(organization)

Cherian, A., and S.V. Thomas. 2009. "Status Epilepticus." *Annals of Indian Academy of Neurology* 12, no. 3, 140–53. http://doi.org/10.4103/0972-2327. 56312

Cisco. February 3, 2015. "Cisco Visual Networking Index (VIN) Mobile Forecast Projects Nearly 1fold Global Mobile Data Traffic Growth Over Next Five Years." http://investor.cisco.com/investor-relations/news-and-events/news/news-details/2015/Cisco-Visual-Networking-Index-VNI-Mobile-Forecast-Projects-Nearly-10-Fold-Global-Mobile-Data-Traffic-Growth-Over-Next-Five-Years/default.aspx

Claeys, A.S., and V. Cauberghe. 2012. "Crisis Response and Crisis Timing Strategies, Two Sides of the Same Coin." *Public Relations Review* 38, no. 1, pp. 83–88.

Coats, T. 2016. *A Single Beat.* Capstrat video (internal).

Cohn, D., and A. Caumont. March 31, 2016. "10 Demographic Trends that are Shaping the U.S. and the World." http://pewresearch.org/fact-tank/2016/03/31/10-demographic-trends-that-are-shaping-the-u-s-and-the-world/

CompTIA. 2016. *Cyberstates 2016.* https://comptia.org/resources/cyberstates-2016

Confino, J. November 5, 2012. "Business Warned to Prepare for Catastrophic Impacts." *The Guardian.* http://theguardian.com/sustainable-business/blog/pwc-climate-change-reduction-business-investments

Constine, J., and A. Escher. May 27, 2015. "The Mary Meeker Internet Trends 2015 Report." *Internet Trends 2015.*

Coombs, W.T. 2007. "Protecting Organization Reputations During a Crisis: The Development and Application of Situational Crisis Communication Theory." *Corporate Reputation Review* 10, no. 3, pp. 163–76.

Coombs, W.T., and S.J. Holladay. 2002. "Helping Crisis Managers Protect Reputational Assets Initial Tests of the Situational Crisis Communication Theory." *Management Communication Quarterly* 16, no. 2, pp. 165–86.

Coombs, W.T., and S.J. Holladay. 2005. "An Exploratory Study of Stakeholder Emotions: Affect and Crises." *Research on Emotion in Organizations* 1, pp. 263–80.

Coombs, W.T. 2017. *Ongoing Crisis Communication: Planning, Managing, and Responding,* 4th ed. Beverley Hills, CA: Sage.

Cutlip, S.M., and A.H. Center. 1971. *Effective Public Relations,* 4th ed. Englewood Cliffs, NJ: Prentice-Hall.

Cutlip, S.M. 1995. *Public Relations History: From the 17th to the 20th Century.* Hillsdale, NJ: Lawrence Erlbaum.

Daft, R.L., and D. Marcic. 2013. *Building Management Skills: An Action-First Approach.* Cengage Learning.

Deloitte. 2008. *Stakeholder Engagement.* https://deloitte.com/content/dam/Deloitte/za/Documents/governance-risk-compliance/ZA_StakeholderEngagement_04042014.pdf

Deloitte. 2014. "Global Human Capital Trends 2014." http://dupress.com/wp-content/uploads/2014/04/GlobalHumanCapitalTrends_2014.pdf

Deloitte. 2015. "Technology and People: The Great Job-Creating Machine." https://deloitte.com/content/dam/Deloitte/uk/Documents/finance/deloitte-uk-technology-and-people.pdf

Dutton, J.E., and W.J. Penner. 1993. "The Importance of Organizational Identity for Strategic Agenda Building." In *Strategic Thinking: Leadership and the Management of Change,* eds. J. Hendry, G. Johnson, and J. Newton, 89–113. Chichester, UK: John Wiley.

Edelman. 2016. "2016 Edelman Trust Barometer." http://edelman.com/insights/intellectual-property/2016-edelman-trust-barometer/

Edelman. January 15, 2017. "2017 Edelman Trust Barometer Reveals Global Implosion of Trust." http://edelman.com/news/2017-edelman-trust-barometer-reveals-global-implosion/

Environmental Protection Agency. n.d. "The National Environmental Policy Act of 1969." https://epa.gov/nepa

EY and Boston College Center for Corporate Citizenship. 2013. "Value of Sustainability Reporting." http://ey.com/Publication/vwLUAssets/EY_-_Value_of_sustainability_reporting/$FILE/EY-Value-of-Sustainability-Reporting.pdf

Fiksel, J., T. Eason, and H. Frederickson. October 2012. *A Framework for Sustainability Indicators at EPA*. Washington, DC: Environmental Protection Agency. https://epa.gov/sites/production/files/2014-10/documents/framework-for-sustainability-indicators-at-epa.pdf

Fombrun, C.J. 1996. *Reputation: Realizing Value From the Corporate Image*. Boston, MA: Harvard Business School Press.

Ford, M. 2015. *The Rise of the Robots: Technology and the Threat of a Jobless Future*. New York, NY: Basic Books.

Forrestal, D.J. 1977. *Faith, Hope & $5,000: The Story of Monsanto, Trials and Triumphs of the First 75 Years*. New York, NY: Simon and Schuster.

Freeman, R.E. 1984. *Strategic Management: A Stakeholder Approach*. Boston, MA: Pitman.

Freeman, R.E., and D.L. Reed. 1884. "Stockholders and Stakeholders: A New Perspective on Corporate Governance." *California Management Review* 25, no. 3, pp. 88–106.

French, W., and A. Weis. 2000. "An Ethics of Care or an Ethics of Justice." *Journal of Business Ethics* 27, no. 1, pp. 125–36.

Friedman, M. September 13, 1970. "The Social Responsibility of Business Is to Increase Profits." *New York Times Magazine*, pp. 122–26.

Freeman, R.E. 1984. *Strategic Management: A Stakeholder Approach*. Cambridge, UK: Cambridge University Press.

Frost, M.D. March 25, 2011. Letter to author Sally Benjamin Young.

Fry. R. April 25, 2016. *Millennials Overtake Baby Boomers as America's Largest Generation*. Pew Research Center. http://pewresearch.org/fact-tank/2016/04/25/millennials-overtake-baby-boomers/

Fundacion DARA Internacional. 2012. *Climate Vulnerability Monitor*, 2nd ed. http://daraint.org/wp-content/uploads/2012/09/CVM2ndEd-FrontMatter.pdf

Gadiesh, O., and J.L. Gilbert. 2001. "Transforming Corner-Office Strategy into Frontline Action." *Harvard Business Review*. Retrieved April 24, 2016, from https://hbr.org/2001/05/transforming-corner-office-strategy-into-frontline-action

Gartner. August 22, 2014. "Gartner Says Worldwide Information Security Spending Will Grow Almost 8 Percent in 2014 as Organizations Become More Threat Aware." http://gartner.com/newsroom/id/2828722

Gartner. September 29, 2016. *Gartner Says Connected Car Production to Grow Rapidly Over Next Five Years.* Forecast: Connected Car Production, Worldwide. http://gartner.com/newsroom/id/3460018

Gitman, L., and S. Enright. April 2, 2015. "Breakthroughs in Stakeholder Engagement." *Business Social Responsibility* (BSR). http://bsr.org/en/our-insights/blog-view/breakthroughs-in-stakeholder-engagement

Glassdoor. January 2016. "Glassdoor U.S. Site Survey." Retrieved January 2016 from https://glassdoor.com/employers/popular-topics/hr-stats.htm (website no longer available).

Golden, L.L.L. 1967. "Public Relations Lessons of History." *Saturday Review.* July 8.

Goodpaster, K.E. 2007. *Conscience and Corporate Culture.* Hoboken, NJ: Blackwell.

Google Search Statistics. n.d. http://internetlivestats.com/google-search-statistics/. Retrieved 10/5/2017.

Greyser, S.A. May 2008. "Authenticity and Reputation." Paper presented at Tuck School of Business (Dartmouth College) Corporate Communications Seminar.

Greyser, S.A. 2009. "Corporate Brand Reputation and Brand Crisis Management." *Management Decision* 47, no. 4, pp. 590–602.

Greyser, S.A., and S.L. Diamond. 1974. "Business is Adapting to Consumerism." *Harvard Business Review* 52, no. 5, pp. 38–58.

Global Reporting Initiative and Carbon Disclosure Project. n.d. http://database.globalreporting.org/ Global Reporting Initiative https://globalreporting.org/resourcelibrary/Linking-GRI-And-CDP.pdf

GMA Intelligence. n.d. "Definitive Data and Analysis for the Mobile Industry." https://gsmaintelligence.com/ (n.d.). Retrieved 10/5/2017.

Griese, N.L. 2001. *Arthur W. Page: Publisher, Public Relations Pioneer, Patriot.* Manila, Phillipines: Anvil Publishing.

Grunig, J.E. 1987. "Symmetrical Presuppositions as a Framework for Public Relations Theory." A Paper Presented to the Conference on Communication Theory and Public Relations, Illinois State University, Normal, Illinois.

Grunig, J.E. 1992a. "What Is Excellence in Management?" In *Excellence in Public Relations and Communication Management*, ed. J.E. Grunig, 219–50. Hillsdale, NJ: Lawrence Erlbaum Associates.

Grunig, J.E. 1992b. "Symmetrical Systems of Internal Communication." In *Excellence in Public Relations and Communication Management*, ed. J.E. Grunig, 531–75. Hillsdale, NJ: Lawrence Erlbaum Associates.

Grunig, J.E. 2006. "Furnishing the Edifice: Ongoing Research on Public Relations as a Strategic Management Function." *Journal of Public Relations Research* 18, no. 2, pp. 151–76.

Grunig, J.E. 2011. "Public Relations and Strategic Management: Institutionalizing Organization-Public Relations in Contemporary Society." *Central European Journal of Communication* 1, no. 4, pp. 11–30.

Grunig, J.E., and T. Hunt. 1984. *Managing Public Relations.* New York, NY: Hold, Rinehart and Winston.

Grunig, L.A., J.E. Grunig, and D.M. Dozier. 2002. *Excellent Public Relations and Effective Organizations: A Study of Communication Management in Three Countries.* Mahwah, NJ: Lawrence Erlbaum.

GSMA. 2015. "The Mobile Economy." http://gsmamobileeconomy.com/ GSMA_Global_Mobile_Economy_Report_2015.pdf

Harrison, E.B., and J. Mühlberg. 2014. *Leadership Communication: How Leaders Communicate and How Communicators Lead in the Today's Global Enterprise.* New York, NY: Business Expert Press.

Harvard School of Public Health & World Economic Forum. September 2011. "The Global Economic Burden of Non-Communicable Diseases." http://weforum.org/docs/WEF_Harvard_HE_GlobalEconomic BurdenNonCommunicableDiseases_2011.pdf

Heath, R.L. 2006. "A Rhetorical Theory Approach to Issues Management." In *Public Relations Theory II,* eds. C. Botan and V. Hazelton. Mahwah, NJ: Lawrence Erlbaum.

Hendricks, D. March 2015. "Now that Software's Eaten the World, It's Started to Eat the Company. Inc." http://inc.com/drew-hendricks/now-that-software-s-eaten-the-world-it-s-started-to-eat-the-company.html

Henige, M.T. 1993. *The Influence of Paul Garrett on General Motors Public Relations and the Development of Corporate PR.* Master of Arts thesis, Wayne State University.

Henige, M.T.R. 1995. "General Motors Paul Garrett—PR's First Industrial Company VP." *PRSA Detroit,* 7–8. http://gmprhistory.com/content/dam/ Media/microsites/product/paul_garrett/pdf/Garrett_PRSA_Article.pdf

Hirsch, L.J. April 29, 2011. Letter to author Sally Benjamin Young.

Holmes Report. 2016. "Global Communication Report 2016." http:// holmesreport.com/docs/default-source/default-document-library/2016-global-communication-report.pdf?sfvrsn=2

IBM. 2016a. "11th Annual Cost of Data Breach Study." http://www-03.ibm. com/security/data-breach/

IBM. 2016b. "2016 Cyber Security Intelligence Index." http://www-03.ibm. com/security/data-breach/cyber-security-index.html

IBM. 2016c. *Bringing Big Data to the Enterprise.* https://www-01.ibm.com/ software/data/bigdata/what-is-big-data.html

IBM. 2016d. "IBM CEO Ginni Rometty's Letter to the U.S. President-Elect." https://ibm.com/blogs/policy/ibm-ceo-ginni-romettys-letter-u-s-president-elect/

IDC Worldwide Quarterly Wearable Device Tracker Data Reported in IDC Press Release. June 21, 2017. "Business Wire." http://businesswire.com/news/home/20170621005129/en/Worldwide-Wearables-Market-Double-2021-IDC/

Institute for Public Relations. May 6, 2016. "Organizational Clarity: The Case for Workplace Alignment and Belief." http://instituteforpr.org/wp-content/uploads/Organizational-Clarity-White-Paper-05-06-16-Final-Online.pdf

Internetlivestats.com. June 30, 2016. Live Stats. http://internetlivestats.com/one-second/

Iwata, J., and S. O'Neill. March 14, 2016. *A Look into the Future: The New CCO*. Arthur W. Page Society. http://awpagesociety.com/blog/a-look-into-the-future-the-new-cco

Jablin, F.M. 1987. "Formal Organization Structure." In *Handbook of Organizational Communication: An Interdisciplinary Perspective*, eds. F.M. Jablin, L.L. Putnam, K.H. Roberts, and L.W. Porter, 389–419. Newbury Park, CA: Sage.

Kah Leng, L. May 20, 2016. "Mobile Commerce to Continue Rapid Growth in 2016." *The Star*. http://thestar.com.my/tech/tech-news/2016/05/20/mobile-commerce-to-continue-rapid-growth-in-2016/

Kanter, R.M. November 2011. "How Great Companies Think Differently." *Harvard Business Review*. https://hbr.org/2011/11/how-great-companies-think-differently/ar/1

Korn Ferry Institute. 2012. "The Chief Communication Officer: Korn/Ferry's 2012 Survey of Fortune 500 Companies." http://kornferryinstitute.com/sites/all/files/documents/briefings-magazinedownload/KF_CCOSurvey12.pdf

KPMG. 2015. "Global CEO Outlook 2015." https://kpmg.com/Global/en/IssuesAndInsights/ArticlesPublications/ceo-outlook/Documents/global-ceo-outlook-2015-v2.pdf

Li, C., and D.W. Stacks. 2015. *Is Social Media Needed To Profit In Business? A Fortune 500 Perspective*. New York, NY: Peter Lang.

Lundbeck A/S, H. 2011. *Lundbeck Overhauls Pentobarbital Distribution to Restrict Misuse* [press release]. Retrieved from http://investor.lundbeck.com/releasedetail.cfm?ReleaseID=605775

Matin, H.Z., G. Jandaghi, F.H. Karimi, and A. Hamidizadeh. 2010. "Relationship Between Interpersonal Communication Skills and Organizational Commitment (Case Study: Jahad Keshavarzi and University of Qom, Iran)." *European Journal of Social Sciences* 13, no. 3, pp. 387–98.

Matos Marques Simoes, P., and M. Esposito. 2014. "Improving Change Management: How Communication Nature Influences Resistance to Change." *Journal of Management Development* 33, no. 4, pp. 324–41.

McCarthy, C. May 26, 2016. "Types of Stakeholders." *Organizational Communications*. Retrieved July 14, 2016. https://boundless.com/users/14854/textbooks/organizational-communications/introduction-to-organizational-communications-1/introduction-to-organizational-communications-2/types-of-stakeholders-12-13355/

McKinsey Global Institute. June 2012. "The World at Work: Jobs, Pay, and Skills for 3.5 Billion People." http://mckinsey.com/global-themes/employment-and-growth/the-world-at-work

McKinsey & Company. July 2014. "Sustainability's Strategic Worth: McKinsey Global Survey *Results*." http://mckinsey.com/business-functions/sustainability-and-resource-productivity/our-insights/sustainabilitys-strategic-worth-mckinsey-global-survey-results

McKinsey & Company. January 2015. "Why Diversity Matters." http://mckinsey.com/business-functions/organization/our-insights/why-diversity-matters

McPhee, R.D., and M.S. Poole. 2001. "Organizational Structures and Configurations." In *The New Handbook of Organizational Communication: Advances in Theory, Research, and Methods*, eds. F.M. Jablin and L.L. Putnam, 503–43. Thousand Oaks, CA: Sage.

Mekonnen, M.M., and A.Y. Hoekstra. February 12, 2016. "Four Billion People Facing Severe Water Scarcity." http://advances.sciencemag.org/content/2/2/e1500323

Men, R.L., and W.H.S. Tsai. 2015. "Infusing Social Media with Humanity: Corporate Character, Public Engagement, and Relational Outcomes." *Public Relations Review* 41, no. 3, pp. 395–403.

Men, R.L., and S.A. Bowen. 2017. *Excellence in Internal Relations Management*. New York, NY: Business Expert Press.

Michaelson, D., and D.W. Stacks. 2017. *A Professional and Practitioner's Guide to Public Relations Research, Measurement, and Evaluation*, 3rd ed. New York, NY: Business Expert Press.

Miller, D.W., and T. Ewest. 2013. "Rethinking the Impact of Religion on Business Values: Understanding its Reemergence and Measuring its Manifestations." *Dimensions of Teaching Business Ethics in Asia*, 29–38. doi:10.1007/978-3-642-36022-0_3

Moore, G. 2015. "Corporate Character, Corporate Virtues." *Business Ethics: A European Review* 24, no. S2, pp. S99–S114.

Morgan, S. July 9, 2015. "Worldwide Cybersecurity Market Continues its Upward Trend." http://csoonline.com/article/2946017/security-leadership/worldwide-cybersecurity-market-sizing-and-projections.html

Mukherjee, A., and H. He. 2008. "Company Identity and Marketing: An Integrative Framework." *Journal of Marketing Theory and Practice* 16, no. 2, pp. 111–25.

Neil, J. 2009. "Stakeholder." http://investopedia.com/terms/s/stakeholder.asp

New York Times. October 30, 2013. "Lawrence Foster." http://nytimes.com/2013/10/30/business/lawrence-g-foster-dies-at-88-helped-lead-tylenol-out-of-cyanide-crisis.html

PatientView Ltd. 2016. *The Corporate Reputation of Pharma—The Patient Perspective in 2015* (US Edition). London, UK.

Perrin, A. "Fact Tank: One-fifth of Americans report going online 'almost constantly.'" October 8, 2015. http://pewresearch.org/fact-tank/2015/12/08/one-fifth-of-americans-report-going-online-almost-constantly/

Pew Research Center. June 29, 2009. "Growing Old in America: Expectations vs. Reality." http://pewsocialtrends.org/2009/06/29/growing-old-in-america-expectations-vs-reality/

Pew Research Center. September 16, 2014. "Faith and Skepticism About Trade, Foreign Investment." http://pewglobal.org/2014/09/16/faith-and-skepticism-about-trade-foreign-investment/

Pew Research Center. October 8, 2015. "Social Media Usage: 2005–2015." http://pewinternet.org/2015/10/08/social-networking-usage-2005-2015/

Pew Research Center. 2015, April 15. "Cell Phones in Africa: Communication Lifeline." http://pewglobal.org/2015/04/15/cell-phones-in-africa-communication-lifeline/

Pew Research Center. April 2, 2015. "The Future of World Religions: Population Growth Projections, 2010–2050." http://pewforum.org/2015/04/02/religious-projections-2010-2050/

Pew Research Center. August 5, 2015. "Across Racial Lines, More Say Nation Needs to Make Changes to Achieve Racial Equality." http://people-press.org/2015/08/05/across-racial-lines-more-say-nation-needs-to-make-changes-to-achieve-racial-equality/

Pew Research Center. January 20, 2016. "Fact Tank: More Americans Using Smartphones for Getting Directions, Streaming TV." http://pewresearch.org/fact-tank/2016/01/29/us-smartphone-use/

Pew Research Center. June 26, 2015. "Gay Marriage Around the World." http://pewforum.org/2015/06/26/gay-marriage-around-the-world-2013/

Pew Research Center. February 22, 2016. "Smartphone Ownership and Internet Usage Continues to Climb in Emerging Economies." http://pewglobal.org/2016/02/22/smartphone-ownership-and-internet-usage-continues-to-climb-in-emerging-economies/v

Pew Research Center. June 13, 2016. "Europeans Face the World Divided." http://pewglobal.org/2016/06/13/europeans-face-the-world-divided/

Pew Research Center. June 27, 2016. "On Views of Race and Inequality, Blacks and Whites are Worlds Apart." http://pewsocialtrends.org/2016/06/27/on-views-of-race-and-inequality-blacks-and-whites-are-worlds-apart/

Pew Research Center. December 19, 2016. "2. Online Reviews." http://pewinternet.org/2016/12/19/online-reviews/

PocketGamer.biz. 2016. "Count of Application Submissions." http://pocketgamer.biz/metrics/app-store/submissions/

Poole, M.S., and R.D. McPhee. 1983. "A Structurational Theory of Organizational Climate." In *Organizational Communication: An Interpretive Approach*, eds. L. Putnam and M. Pacanowski. Newbury Park, CA: Sage.

PRWeek/Brands2Life. 2015. "Communication Directors Study 2015." http://brands2life.com/news/pr-weekbrands2life-communication-directors-study-view-top/?refresh=true

PwC. 2014. "CEO Pulse on Climate Change." http://download.pwc.com/gx/ceo-pulse/climatechange/index.htm

PwC. 2016. "Global CEO Survey: Redefining Business Success in a Changing World." https://pwc.com/gx/en/ceo-survey/2016/landing-page/pwc-19th-annual-global-ceo-survey.pdf

Radnofsky, L. February 4, 2016. "Companies Form New Alliance to Target Health-Care Costs." *Wall Street Journal*. http://wsj.com/articles/companies-form-health-insurance-alliance-1454633281

Recode. April 17, 2017. "Netflix Missed its Q1 Subscriber Numbers but Q2 Looks Better." https://recode.net/2017/4/17/15330738/netflix-q1-earnings-streaming

Reprieve. 2012. "Pharma Firm Lundbeck Wins Ethical Award for Stopping Use of Drugs in Executions [Press Release]." Retrieved from http://reprieve.org.uk/press/2012_03_29_lundbeck_ethical_award/

Ryan, M., and D.L. Martinson. 1988. "Journalists and Public Relations Practitioners: Why the Antagonism?" *Journalism Quarterly* 65, no. 1, pp. 131–40.

Said Business School and Heidrick and Struggles. 2015. "The CEO Report." http://sbs.ox.ac.uk/sites/default/files/Press_Office/Docs/The-CEO-Report-Final.pdf

Sanchez-Cortes, D., O. Aran, D.B. Jayagopi, M.S. Mast, and D. Gatica-Perez. 2013. "Emergent Leaders Through Looking and Speaking: From Audio-Visual Data to Multimodal Recognition." *Journal on Multimodal User Interfaces* 7, nos. 1–2, pp. 39–53.

Schultz, H. 2014. "Howard Schultz: Redefining the Role and Responsibility for a For-Profit, Public Company." https://news.starbucks.com/2014annualmeeting/howard-schultz-2014-shareholders-speech

Seeger, M.W. 1997. *Ethics and Organizational Communication*. Cresskill, NJ: Hampton.

Shin, Y. 2012. "CEO Ethical Leadership, Ethical Climate, Climate Strength, and Collective Organizational Citizenship Behavior." *Journal of Business Ethics* 108, no. 3, pp. 299–312.

Siebold, D.R., and B.C. Shea. 2001. "Participation and Decision Making." In *The New Handbook of Organizational Communication: Advances in Theory, Research, and Methods*, eds. F.M. Jablin and L.L. Putnam, 664–703. Thousand Oaks, CA: Sage.

Siegel, R.P. March 13, 2013. "Top Ten Effects of Global Warming on Business." *Triple Pundit*. http://triplepundit.com/2013/03/top-ten-effects-global-warming-business/#

Simonite, T. May 13, 2016. "Moore's Law is Dead, Now What?" *MIT Technology Review*. https://technologyreview.com/s/601441/moores-law-is-dead-now-what/

Sims, R.R. 1994. *Ethics and Organizational Decision Making: A Call for RENEWAL*. Westport, CT: Quorum.

Smart Insights. February 6, 2017. "With this Much Social Media Activity Every Minute, Content Shock Will Increase as a Challenge for Marketers in 2017." http://smartinsights.com/internet-marketing-statistics/happens-online-60-seconds/

Smircich, L., and M.B. Calas. 1987. "Organizational Culture: A Critical Assessment." In *Handbook of Organizational Communication: An Interdisciplinary Perspective*, eds. F.M. Jablin, L.L. Putnam, K.H. Roberts, and L.W. Porter, 228–63. Newbury Park, CA: Sage.

Southwest Airlines. n.d. "Purpose, Vision, Values, and Mission." http://investors.southwest.com/ourcompany/purpose_vision_values_and_mission

Srinaruewan, P., W. Binney, and C. Higgins. 2015. "Consumer Reactions to Corporate Social Responsibility (CSR) in Thailand: The Moderating Effect of Competitive Positioning." *Asia Pacific Journal of Marketing and Logistics* 27, no. 4, pp. 628–52.

Sriramesh, K., J.E. Grunig, and J. Buffington. 1992. "Corporate Culture and Public Relations." In *Excellence in Public Relations and Communication Management*, ed. J.E. Grunig, 577–95. Hillsdale, NJ: Lawrence Erlbaum Associates.

Stacks, D.W. 2017. *Primer of Public Relations Research*, 3rd ed. New York, NY: Guilford Press.

Stacks, D.W., and S.A. Bowen. 2013. *Dictionary of Public Relations Research and Measurement*. Gainesville, FL: Institute for Public Relations. http://instituteforpr.org/dictionary-public-relations-measurement-research-third-edition/

Stacks, D.W., M.L. Hickson, and S.R. Hill. 1991. *An Introduction To Communication Theory*. Dallas, TX: Holt, Rinehart & Winston.

Standish, P. 2012. "This is Produced by a Brain Process! Wittgenstein, Transparency in Psychology Today." *Journal of Philosophy of Education* 46, no. 1, pp. 60–72.

Synacor. *Annual Report 2015*. http://files.shareholder.com/downloads/SYNC/2306383171x0x885039/CAB8A0FF-1A95-4CEB-B12D-B5F35020DF7A/SYNC_AR.pdfThe Public Disputes Program (n.d.). http://web.mit.edu/publicdisputes/pdr/

The Altimeter Group. July 28, 2015. "The 2015 State of Social Business." http://altimetergroup.com/pdf/reports/2015-State-Of-Social-Business-Altimeter-Group.pdf

The Economist. December 13, 2014. "The Openness Revolution." http://economist.com/news/business/21636070-multinationals-are-forced-reveal-more-about-themselves-where-should-limits

The Economist. March 12, 2016. "Technology Quarterly: After Moore's Law." http://economist.com/technology-quarterly/2016-03-12/after-moores-law

The World Bank. 2014. "The Global Findex Database 2014: Measuring Financial Inclusion Around the World." http://worldbank.org/en/programs/globalfindex

Tierney, J. May 17, 2014. "How to Win Millennials: Equality, Climate Change, and Gay Marriage." *Atlantic Magazine.* http://theatlantic.com/politics/archive/2014/05/everything-you-need-to-know-about-millennials-political-views/371053/

Trevino, L.K. 1986. "Ethical Decision Making in Organizations: A Person Situation Interactionist Model." *Academy of Management Review* 11, no. 3, pp. 601–17.

Trevino, L.K., G.R. Weaver, and S.J. Reynolds. 2006. "Behavioral Ethics in Organizations: A Review." *Journal of Management* 32, no. 6, pp. 951–90.

UN Global Compact. 2016. "The CEO Water Mandate." http://ceowatermandate.org/why-stewardship/stewardship-is-good-for-business/

UN Global Compact-Accenture. 2013. "UN Global Compact: Accenture CEO Study on Sustainability 2013." https://accenture.com/us-en/insight-un-global-compact-ceo-study-sustainability

UN Women. 2015. "Facts and Figures: Economic Empowerment." http://unwomen.org/en/what-we-do/economic-empowerment/facts-and-figures

UNDESA (United Nations Department of Economic and Social Affairs). 2015. *International Decade for Action "water for life" 2005–2015.* http://un.org/waterforlifedecade/human_right_to_water.shtml

United Nations. 2015. "Sustainable Development Goals." http://undp.org/content/undp/en/home/sdgoverview/post-2015-development-agenda.html

Urde, M., S.A. Greyser, and J.M.T. Balmer. 2007. "Corporate Brands with a Heritage." *Journal of Brand Management* 15, no. 1, pp. 4–19.

Urde, M 2009. "Uncovering the Corporate Brand's Core Values." *Management Decision* 47, no. 4, pp. 616–38.

USC Annenberg. 2016. "Global Communications Report: Executive Summary." http://annenberg.usc.edu/sites/default/files/USC_REPORT_New.pdf

Valukas, A.R. May 29, 2014. "Report to the Board of Directors of General Motors Company Regarding Ignition Switch Recalls." http://beasleyallen.com/webfiles/valukas-report-on-gm-redacted.pdf

Vlasic, B. June 5, 2014. "G.M. Inquiry Cites Years of Neglect Over Fatal Defect." *The New York Times.* https://nytimes.com/2014/06/06/business/gm-ignition-switch-internal-recall-investigation-report.html

Volf, M. 2016. *Flourishing: Why We Need Religion in a Globalized World.* New Haven, CT: Yale University Press.

Volk, S.C., and A. Zerfass. May 2017. "Alignment: Revisiting a Key Concept in Strategic Communication." Paper Presented at the International Communication Association Annual Conference, San Diego, CA.

Weber Shandwick. 2014. "The Rising CCO V: Chief Communications Officers' Perspectives on a Changing Media Environment." *Newsroom.* http://weber shandwick.com/news/article/the-rising-cco-v-chief-communications-officers-perspectives-changing-media

webpagefx.com. June 30, 2016. "The Internet in Real Time." http://webpagefx. com/internet- real-time/

Welch, J. 1981. "1981 GE Annual Report to Shareholders." https://callcentres. com.au/GE5_Jack_Welch.htm

Wheelan, S.A. 2014. *Creating Effective Teams: A Guide for Members and Leaders.* Sage Publications.

White House. April 2015. "Gender Pay Gap: Recent Trends and Explanations." https://whitehouse.gov/sites/default/files/docs/equal_pay_issue_brief_final. pdf

World Economic Forum. 2015. "Executive opinion Survey 2014." http://reports. weforum.org/global-risks-2015/executive-opinion-survey-2014/

World Health Organization. 2009. "Global Health risks." http://who.int/ healthinfo/global_burden_disease/GlobalHealthRisks_report_full.pdf

World Health Organization. 2016. "Water Sanitation Health." http://who.int/ water_sanitation_health/wsh0404summary/en/

About the Authors

Paul Argenti is Professor of Corporate Communication in the Tuck School of Business at Dartmouth.

Mark Bain is President of upper 90 consulting and a former CCO.

Roger Bolton is President of the Arthur W. Page Society, a former CCO at Aetna Inc., and U.S. Department of the Treasury, and a former Chair of the Arthur W. Page Society.

Shannon A. Bowen is Professor in College of Information and Communications, School of Mass Communications and Information Studies, University of South Carolina.

W. Timothy Coombs is Professor in the Department of Communication, Texas A&M University.

Marcia DiStaso is Associate Professor and Chair in the Department of Public Relations, College of Journalism and Mass Communication, University of Florida.

Richard Edelman is President and Chief Executive Officer of Edelman and an inductee into the Arthur W. Page Society Hall of Fame.

Bob Feldman is a partner and cofounder of PulsePoint Group and a former CCO.

Michael Fernandez is U.S. CEO of Burson-Marsteller and a former CCO.

Terence (Terry) Flynn is Associate Professor and Lead Professor, Master of Communications Management (MCM) Degree Program in the Department of Communication Studies & Multimedia, McMaster University.

Matthew Gonring is Principal, MP Gonring Associates, and a former CCO.

Stephen A. Greyser is Richard P. Chapman Professor (Marketing/Communications) *Emeritus*, Harvard Business School.

Ginger Hardage is retired, Senior Vice President, Culture and Communications, Southwest Airlines.

E. Bruce Harrison is Counselor, Faculty *Emeritus*, Georgetown University, a former CCO, and a recipient of the Arthur W. Page Society Distinguished Service Award.

Aedhmar Hynes is CEO, Text100, 2018 Chair of the Arthur W. Page Society, and a recipient of the Arthur W. Page Society Distinguished Service Award.

Jon Iwata is formerly Chief Brand Officer, IBM Corporation, former Chair of the Arthur W. Page Society, and an inductee into the Arthur W. Page Society Hall of Fame.

Raymond Kotcher is Non-Executive Chairman of Ketchum and Professor of the Practice, College of Communication, Boston University, and an inductee into the Arthur W. Page Society Hall of Fame.

Maril MacDonald is Founder and CEO, Gagen MacDonald, a former CCO, a recipient of the Arthur W. Page Society Distinguished Service Award and former Chair of the Arthur W. Page Society.

Alan Marks is Chief Communications Officer, ServiceNow.

Tom Martin is Executive-in-Residence, Department of Communication, College of Charleston, a former CCO, a recipient of the Arthur W. Page

Society Distinguished Service Award, and former Chair of the Arthur W. Page Society.

Tina McCorkindale is President and CEO of the Institute for Public Relations.

Eliot Mizrachi is Vice President, Communications and Thought Leadership, Arthur W. Page Society.

Sean O'Neill is a former Heineken CCO (2004-2016) and co-Chair of the 2016 Arthur W. Page Society Report, "The New CCO: Transforming Enterprises in a Changing World."

James S. O'Rourke, IV, is Professor and Director, The Eugene D. Fanning Center, University of Notre Dame, and a recipient of the Arthur W. Page Society Distinguished Service Award.

Charlotte R. Otto is a former CCO and an inductee into the Arthur W. Page Society Hall of Fame.

Jennifer Prosek is CEO and Founder, Prosek Partners.

David Samson is General Manager, Public Affairs, Chevron Corporation, and 2016 to 2018 Chair of the Arthur W. Page Society.

Gary Sheffer is a former CCO, Senior Corporate Strategist, Weber Shandwick, and former Chair of the Arthur W. Page Society.

James Spangler is Vice President, Corporate Affairs and Chief Communications Officer, Navistar International, Inc.

Don W. Stacks is Professor *Emeritus*, Department of Strategic Communication, School of Communication, University of Miami.

Wendi Strong is retired, Executive Vice President for Enterprise Affairs and Chief Communications Officer, USAA.

Richard Woods is Senior Vice President, Corporate Affairs, Capital One Financial Corporation.

Donald K. Wright is Harold Burson Professor and Chair in Public Relations, College of Communication, Boston University, and a recipient of the Arthur W. Page Society Distinguished Service Award.

Sally Benjamin Young is Vice President, Public Affairs, Lundbeck.

Index

OTHER TITLES IN OUR PUBLIC RELATIONS COLLECTION

Don W. Stacks and Donald K. Wright, Editors

- *Excellence in Internal Communication Management* by Rita Linjuan Men and Shannon A. Bowen
- *A Professional and Practitioner's Guide to Public Relations Research, Measurement, and Evaluation, Third Edition* by David Michaelson and Donald W. Stacks
- *A Communication Guide for Investor Relations in an Age of Activism* by Marcia W. DiStaso, David Michaelson, and John Gilfeather
- *Corporate Communication Crisis Leadership: Advocacy and Ethics* by Ronald C. Arnett, Sarah M. Deluliis, and Matthew Corr
- *Public Relations Ethics: Senior PR Pros Tell Us How to Speak Up and Keep Your Job* by Marlene S. Neill and Amy Oliver Barnes

Announcing the Business Expert Press Digital Library

Concise e-books business students need for classroom and research

This book can also be purchased in an e-book collection by your library as

- a one-time purchase,
- that is owned forever,
- allows for simultaneous readers,
- has no restrictions on printing, and
- can be downloaded as PDFs from within the library community.

Our digital library collections are a great solution to beat the rising cost of textbooks. E-books can be loaded into their course management systems or onto students' e-book readers.
The **Business Expert Press** digital libraries are very affordable, with no obligation to buy in future years. For more information, please visit **www.businessexpertpress.com/librarians**. To set up a trial in the United States, please email **sales@businessexpertpress.com**.

CPSIA information can be obtained
at www.ICGtesting.com
Printed in the USA
LVOW10s2003020318

568482LV00012B/668/P